"Boss S[...]
Sports Sciences
&
Physical Education
Entrance Examination

"Boss Series"
Sports Sciences
&
Physical Education
Entrance Examination

Dr. M.M.S. Bedi

Dr. Meenu Dhingra

PEEPEE
PUBLISHERS and DISTRIBUTORS (P) LTD.

"Boss Series" Sports Sciences & Physical Education
Entrance Examination

Published by
Pawaninder P. Vij
Peepee Publishers and Distributors (P) Ltd.
Head Office: 160, Shakti Vihar, Pitam Pura,
Delhi-110 034
Corporate Office: 7/31, Ansari Road, Daryaganj,
Post Box-7243, New Delhi-110002 (India)
Ph: 55195868, 9811156083
e-mail: peepee160@yahoo.co.in
e-mail: peepee160@rediffmail.com
www.peepeepub.com

This book has been published in good faith that the material provided by authors is original. Every effort is made to ensure accuracy of material, but publisher and printer will not be held responsible for any inadvertent errors. In case of any dispute, all legal matters to be settled under Delhi jurisdiction only.

First Edition: **2005**

ISBN: 81-88867-46-2

Printed at
Lordson, C-5/19, Rana Pratap Bagh, Delhi-110 007

Preface

It is matter of great satisfaction and immense pleasure to present this book, though small in size and yet large enough in terms of contents and quality, to young aspirants who intends to join physical education and sports sciences as a career. The book has been compiled after a close scrutiny of various competitive books and feedback received from the candidates. An effort has been made to cover all types of questions that a candidate may face in their entrance examination. In compiling this book, we had constantly consulted several books and magazines, and hereby acknowledge our indebtedness to all those sources.

We wish to put on record our appreciation for the valuable suggestions provided by Dr Rita Jain, Lecturer, Sports Sciences, University of Delhi.

We are thankful to Mr. Pawaninder Vij, Peepee Publishers and Distributors (P) Ltd., New Delhi-110002 for their thorough in-house review and service to publish this book.

We are also thankful to the students, who have been a constant source of encourgement to prepare this book.

Finally, we always consider the importance of readers who are our best guide. We welcome their suggestions and positive feedback for further improvement of successive editions.

Dr M.M.S. Bedi
Dr Meenu Dhingra

Contents

Chapter one

Boss Series

General Knowledge

Q.1. The Magna Carta is the name of which document?
Ans. A historical document curbing the king's power.

Q.2. Who wrote the communist manifesto?
Ans. Karl Marx.

Q.3. What is Boston tea party associated with?
Ans. American independence.

Q.4. In which year was Bangladesh created?
Ans. 1971.

Q.5. Who emerged as a great leader in France as a result of the French Revolution?
Ans. Napoleon Bonaparte.

Q.6. Who led the Russian Revolution of 1917?
Ans. Lenin.

Q.7. When was the first atom bomb dropped in Hiroshima?
Ans. Aug 6, 1945.

Q.8. Why is red light used in traffic signals?
Ans. Its largest wavelength can be seen from a long distance.

Q.9. **What is the source of solar energy?**
Ans. Nuclear fusion.

Q.10. **Why is food cooked quickly in pressure cooker?**
Ans. Boiling point of water is increased.

Q.11. **What is the use of transformer?**
Ans. To increase or decrease AC voltage.

Q.12. **Where does embryo develop in mammals?**
Ans. Uterus.

Q.13. **How can one determine the age of a tree?**
Ans. By counting the number of rings in the stem.

Q.14. **Which Union Territory of India is the most densely populated?**
Ans. Delhi.

Q.15. **Indian Railways are divided into how many zones?**
Ans. Nine zones.

Q.16. **Which is the maximum percentage of tribal population in India?**
Ans. Santhals.

Q.17. **Where is the 'Black Pagoda'?**
Ans. Konark.

Q.18. **Where is Amarnath located?**
Ans. Jammu and Kashmir.

Q.19. **What is Mount Abu in Rajasthan famous for?**
Ans. Dilwara Temples.

Q.20. **Which is the biggest city of India?**
Ans. Mumbai.

Q.21. **The Hirakud Project on the Mahanadi is located in which state?**
Ans. Orissa.

Q.22. What is Nepanagar in Madhya Pradesh famous for?
Ans. Newsprint paper.

Q.23. What is the shape of Earth's orbit around the sun?
Ans. Elliptical.

Q.24. The Great Barrier Reef is a
Ans. Coral formation.

Q.25. Macmohan line is the border between
Ans. India and China.

Q.26. When the days and nights are equal, where does the rays of the sun directly fall?
Ans. On the Equator.

Q.27. What is the new name for Rhodesia?
Ans. Zimbabwe.

Q.28. The term third world refers to
Ans. Underdeveloped and developing countries.

Q.29. Who is normally the ex-officio chairman of the Planning Commission of India?
Ans. Prime Minister of India.

Q.30. When was Reserve Bank of India established?
Ans. April 1, 1935.

Q.31. Who was the first Indian Governor?
Ans. CD Deshmukh (1943-49).

Q.32. In which bank a personal account cannot be opened?
Ans. Reserve Bank of India.

Q.33. Between which two cities will a bus ply across the line of control w.e.f. April 7, 2005?
Ans. Srinagar-Muzaffarabad.

Q.34. Who Indian figures among a number of distinguished people nominated for the Nobel Peace Prize 2006?
Ans. Pandit Ravi Shankar.

Q.35. Which medium range surface to air missile was test fired recently?

Ans. Akash.

Q.36. Which college of Delhi University joined hands with Lahore's Kinnaired College to provide better opportunities for journalism students?

Ans. Lady Sri Ram College.

Q.37. Which banks got full managerial autonomy by the Centre?

Ans. Public Sector Banks.

Q.38. Which university got 'minority institution status' recently?

Ans. Aligarh Muslim University.

Q.39. Which Bihar governor recently recommended President's rule in the State?

Ans. Mr Buta Singh.

Q.40. Which tax is now being levied in lieu of sales tax?

Ans. Value Added Tax (VAT).

Q.41. Who becomes the world's third wealthiest man according to Forbes 2005 Rich list of Global Billionaires?

Ans. Mr Lakshmi Niwas Mittal.

Q.42. Which NDA leader wins the motion of confidence in Jharkhand recently?

Ans. Arjun Munda.

Q.43. For which film did Satyajit Ray receive his only Filmfare Award as Best Director?

Ans. Shatranj Ke Khiladi.

Q.44. Which Pakistani national won the Best Playback Singer (Female) award in 1982.

Ans. Salma Agha.

Q.45. Who played Elizabeth in Shekhar Kapur's 'Elizabeth'?
Ans. Cate Blanchett.

Q.46. Which Indian won an Oscar for the film 'Gandhi'?
Ans. Bhanu Athaiya.

Q.47. Which film was inspired by seven Brides for seven Brothers?
Ans. Satte Pe Satta.

Q.48. On whose novel was Dev Anand's Guide based?
Ans. R.K. Narayan.

Q.49. Who was the director of the television serial 'Tamas'?
Ans. Govind Nihalani.

Q.50. Which was the first film to win the Filmfare Award for best picture?
Ans. Do Bigha Zamin.

Q.51. Which was the first Indian film to be nominated for an Oscar Award ?
Ans. Mother India.

Q.52. The backdrop of which film is the village of Champaran?
Ans. Lagaan.

Q.53. Which was the first cinemascope film made in India?
Ans. Kagaz Ke Phool.

Q.54. In which film did Aishwarya Rai make her debut?
Ans. Iruvar.

Q.55. Which film lyricist was born in Azamgarh as Akhtar Husain Rizvi?
Ans. Kaifi Azmi.

Q.56. Which Indian actor formed the Majma Theatre group?
Ans. Om Puri.

Q.57. With which film did Javed Akhtar start his carrier as a lyricist?
Ans. Silsila.

Q.58. **Which actress wrote the book 'Eat with me'?**
Ans. Sophia Loren.

Q.59. **What was the name of India's first silent film?**
Ans. Raja Harishchandra.

Q.60. **'Tarkash' is a collection of Urdu poetry by which famous lyricist?**
Ans. Javed Akhtar.

Q.61. **Which script was created by Guru Angad, the second sikh Guru?**
Ans. Gurumukhi.

Q.62. **Which Devarishi was the brother of Riddhi and Siddhi, the twins who married Ganesha?**
Ans. Narada.

Q.63. **What object did Ganesha use to write down the Mahabharta at Vyasa's dictation?**
Ans. His broken tusk.

Q.64. **Which is world's oldest religion?**
Ans. Hinduism.

Q.65. **Which is the largest religion in the world?**
Ans. Christianity.

Q.66. **Which is the sacred text of Buddhism?**
Ans. The Tripitaka.

Q.67. **Which is the main religion of China?**
Ans. Confucianism.

Q.68. **Who was the founder of Ramakrishna Mission?**
Ans. Swami Vivekananda.

Q.69. **Which is the sacred place of Buddhists?**
Ans. Lumbini in Nepal.

Q.70. **Which is the sacred place of Islam?**
Ans. Mecca.

Q.71. Which is the sacred place of Sikhs?
Ans. The Golden Temple of Amritsar.

Q.72. What is the literacy source of Hindu Philosophy?
Ans. The Upanishads.

Q.73. Who founded Jainism?
Ans. Rishabha Dev.

Q.74. In which royal family Mahavira was born?
Ans. Licchavis.

Q.75. At which place did Gautam Buddha deliver his first lecture?
Ans. Sarnath.

Q.76. After assembly elections in February 2005 who is elected as Chief Minister of Haryana?
Ans. Bhupinder Singh Hooda.

Q.77. Other then Goa, in which state President's rule is implemented?
Ans. Bihar.

Q.78. Which bus service has been started across the line of control w.e.f. April 7, 2005?
Ans. Karvan-E-Aman.

Q.79. Between which two cities has Karvan-E-Aman been plied w.e.f. April 7, 2005?
Ans. Srinagar (India) and Muzaffarabad (Pakistan).

Q.80. In which state there is no reservation for SC/ST for Lok Sabha?
Ans. Jammu and Kashmir.

Q.81. Which Indian astronomer adorned the court of Chandra Gupta Vikramaditya?
Ans. Aryabhatta (476-520 AD).

Q.82. Who was the first Indian woman to climb Mt Everest in 1984?
Ans. Bachendri Pal.

Q.83. Who was the founder of Mughal Empire in India?
Ans. Babur (1483-1530).

Q.84. Who is nicknamed as Father of the Indian Constitution?
Ans. B.R. Ambedkar (1893-1956).

Q.85. Which Indian freedom fighter is known as 'Shahid-e-Azam'?
Ans. Bhagat Singh.

Q.86. Who was the last ruler of Mughal Dynasty?
Ans. Bahadur Shah Zafar.

Q.87. Which Sanskrit scholar was a court poet of Harshavardhana?
Ans. Bana Bhatt.

Q.88. Which Indian hockey player has scored maximum goals in Olympic games and has set a record?
Ans. Dhyan Chand.

Q.89. Which famous personality is known as the Lady with the Lamp?
Ans. Florence Nightingale.

Q.90. Which English physicist is famous for his discovery of Laws of Gravitation?
Ans. Sir Issac Newton.

Q.91. Which eminent Indian physicist developed wireless telegraphy?
Ans. J.C. Bose.

Q.92. Which Prime Minister of India was known as the Man of Peace?
Ans. Lal Bahadur Shastri.

Q.93. **Who invented Braille system?**
Ans. Louis Braille.

Q.94. **Who was the first lady of the Indian screen to have nominated to the Rajya Sabha?**
Ans. Nargis Dutt.

Q.95. **Which Hindu King of Punjab, fought against Greek invader Alexander?**
Ans. Porous.

Q.96. **Which Sikh prince earned the title Lion of Punjab?**
Ans. Maharaja Ranjit Singh.

Q.97. **Which social reformer was the founder of Brahmo Samaj?**
Ans. Raja Ram Mohan Roy.

Q.98. **Which poetess is also called 'Nightingale of India'?**
Ans. Sarojini Naidu.

Q.99. **Who was the author of Satyarth Prakash?**
Ans. Swami Dayanand Saraswati.

Q.100. **Which ruler of India was also known as 'India's Napoleon'?**
Ans. Samudragupta.

Q.101. **Who built the wonder of Taj Mahal?**
Ans. Shahjahan.

Q.102. **What is the meaning of tsunami?**
Ans. Harbour wave.

Q.103. **What is the cause of tsunami?**
Ans. By earthquake below or near ocean floors, landslides, volcanic eruption.

Q.104. **Where do most tsunamis occur?**
Ans. Pacific Ocean (Ring of fire).

Q.105. When did tsunami hit recently?
Ans. Dec 26, 2004.

Q.106. What does the tsunami warning system do?
Ans. Issues tsunami warnings to over 100 places across Pacific.

Q.107. Who discovered genes associated with cancer?
Ans. Robert Weinbergin (1982).

Q.108. Who invented bicycle?
Ans. Kirkpatrick Macmillan in (1839-40).

Q.109. Who invented an Aeroplane?
Ans. Orville e.g. Wilbur Wright in 1903.

Q.110. Who invented a Hydrogen Bomb?
Ans. Edward Teller in 1952.

Q.111. Who invented a lightening conductor?
Ans. Benjamin Franklin in 1752.

Q.112. Who invented telephone?
Ans. Alexander Graham Bell.

Q.113. Who invented Gramophone?
Ans. Thomas Alva Edison in 1878.

Q.114. Who discovered X-ray in 1895?
Ans. Roentgen.

Q.115. Which milestone is associated with name of Atreya?
Ans. Discovery of Ayurveda in 2000-1000 B.C.

Q.116. Who discovered Aspirin?
Ans. Dreser in 1889.

Q.117. Who discovered penicillin?
Ans. Alexander Fleming in 1928.

Q.118. Who was successful in making an artificial heart in 1957?
Ans. Willem Kolff.

Q.119. Who discovered the oral poliomyelitis vaccine in 1954?
Ans. Albert Sabin.

Q.120. Who discovered Greenland?
Ans. Eric the Red (He was a Viking).

Q.121. Who discovered the sea route from Europe to India?
Ans. Vaso de-Gama from Portuguese in 1498.

Q.122. Who discovered Canada?
Ans. Jacques Cartier in 1534-36.

Q.123. Which Island Continent was discovered by William Janszoon in 1606?
Ans. Australia.

Q.124. Who discovered Trinidad?
Ans. Christopher Columbus.

Q.125. Who is the chairperson of Congress parliamentary party?
Ans. Ms Sonia Gandhi.

Q.126. Who is the Speaker of Lok Sabha?
Ans. Mr Somnath Chatterjee.

Q.127. Which is the last of the four Vedas?
Ans. Atharva Veda.

Q.128. Who was instrumental in establishing Christianity in India?
Ans. St. Francis Xavier.

Q.129. Of which religion is the Avesta a sacred text?
Ans. Zoroastrianism.

Q.130. Which mystic poet and forerunner of Sikhism established a new religious sect linking Hinduism and Islam?
Ans. Kabir.

Q.131. Who is the 8th incarnation of Lord Vishnu?
Ans. Krishna.

Q.132. Who was Maha Maya?
Ans. Gautam Buddha's mother.

Q.133. Who is the protector and preserver of the world in Hindu mythology?
Ans. Vishnu.

Q.134. Who was the last guru of Sikhs?
Ans. Guru Gobind Singh.

Q.135. Who wrote Ramcharitmanas?
Ans. Tulsi Das.

Q.136. How many couplets the Mahabharata has?
Ans. 1,00,000 couplets.

Q.137. Which Sikh Guru was beheaded in Delhi on Aurangzeb's order?
Ans. Guru Tegh Bahadur.

Q.138. Who created 'Khalsa Panth'?
Ans. Guru Gobind Singh.

Q.139. Who founded the city of Amritsar?
Ans. Guru Ramdas.

Q.140. Which Greek God is often identified with the Roman God Mercury?
Ans. Hermes.

Q.141. How many days are there in a year, as per Islamic Calender?
Ans. 354 days.

Q.142. Who compiled the Granth Sahib, the holy book?
Ans. Guru Arjan Dev.

Q.143. Who is the ruler of the sky realm in Hindu mythology?
Ans. Varuna.

Q.144. Which Hindu God is said to have two faces, one beneficent and one malignant?
Ans. Agni.

Q.145. Who was the founder of Arya Samaj?
Ans. Swami Dayanand Saraswati.

Q.146. Who was the founder of Brahmo Samaj?
Ans. Raja Ram Mohan Roy.

Q.147. Name the gurus who became martyrs of the Sikhs.
Ans. Guru Arjan Dev and Guru Tegh Bahadur.

Q.148. Where did Jain Tirthankar Mahavira died?
Ans. At Pawapuri.

Q.149. In which two sects Jains are divided?
Ans. Shwetambars and Digambars.

Q.150. Which two religions came out strong against the Vedic religion?
Ans. Buddhism and Jainism.

Q.151. Who wrote Ramayana?
Ans. Valmiki.

Q.152. Who is known as 'The Destroyer' in Hindu mythology?
Ans. Shiva.

Q.153. Where was Gautam Buddha born?
Ans. Kapilavastu.

Q.154. Which is the place of worship for Parsis?
Ans. Fire temple.

Q.155. According to the Adhyatma Ravana, who assumed the form of Kali to kill Sahasra-Shirsha Ravana?
Ans. Sita.

Q.156. Which of the eighteen Puranas, named for an eternally youthful sage, contains the 'Devi-Mahatmya'?
Ans. Markandeya Purana.

Q.157. What is the collective term for the incarnate energies of seven Gods who helped Durga against Shumbha and Nishumbha?

Ans. Sapta-Matrikas.

Q.158. Where on the Jabal-an-Noor did the Prophet experience the divine revelation through the angel Jibrail?

Ans. The Cave of Hira.

Q.159. In Greek Myth, which Princess of Troy was a prophetess who was cursed never to be believed?

Ans. Cassandra.

Q.160. From which son of Jacob and Leah is the word 'Jew' derived?

Ans. Judah.

Q.161. Which Muslim sect's name is derived from the Arab word meaning 'tradition'?

Ans. Sunni.

Q.162. To protect which of his devotees did Vishnu assume the Narasimha avatar?

Ans. Prahlada.

Q.163. According to which calendar is Rosh Hashanah celebrated on the first day of Tishri?

Ans. The Jewish Calender.

Q.164. Which Tirthankar's samadhi is at the Jalmandir at Pawapuri?

Ans. Mahavira.

Q.165. Which is the upper House of Parliament called?
Ans. Rajya Sabha.

Q.166. How many members are nominated by the President in Rajya Sabha?
Ans. 12.

Q.167. **Who was the first Chief Minister of Jammu and Kashmir?**
Ans. Sheikh Muhammad Abdullah.

Q.168. **Who was the President of India when Prime Minister Indira Gandhi declared a state of emergency in 1975?**
Ans. Fakhruddin Ali Ahmed.

Q.169. **Who is the only non-Congress PM who had no association with Congress party?**
Ans. Atal Bihari Vajpayee.

Q.170. **In 1969, who became the first President of India to die in office?**
Ans. Zakir Hussain.

Q.171. **Which Congress (I) General-Secretary died in a plane crash in Delhi on 23 June, 1980?**
Ans. Sanjay Gandhi.

Q.172. **Which recognized regional party's symbol is two leaves?**
Ans. AIADMK.

Q.173. **To investigate what was the Thakkar Commission of inquiry set up?**
Ans. The assassination of Indira Gandhi.

Q.174. **Who succeeded Indira Gandhi as president of Congress (I) in 1984?**
Ans. Rajiv Gandhi.

Q.175. **Who was the Chief Minister of Madhya Pradesh at the time of the Bhopal Gas Tragedy in December 1984?**
Ans. Arjun Singh.

Q.176. **Which Congress (I) member of Parliament from Dausa in the thirteenth Lok Sabha died in a road accident?**
Ans. Rajesh Pilot.

Q.177. **Who was the President of the Constituent Assembly?**
Ans. Dr. Rajendra Prasad.

Q.178. Who was the chairman of the Drafting Committee which was appointed to draft the Constitution?
Ans. Dr. B.R. Ambedkar.

Q.179. For how many days constituent assembly met to frame the Constitution?
Ans. 166 days.

Q.180. In which year the word 'Unity and Integrity of the Nation' was added to the preamble of the Constitution?
Ans. 1976.

Q.181. Who is the highest executive authority of India?
Ans. The President.

Q.182. What is the minimum age to be a candidate in President's election in India?
Ans. 35 years.

Q.183. What is the working term for Indian President?
Ans. 5 years.

Q.184. What is the maximum number of members in Rajya Sabha?
Ans. 250.

Q.185. What is the document called which contains policies and programmes of a political party?
Ans. Election Manifesto.

Q.186. What is the 'features of India's foreign policy' known as?
Ans. Panchsheel.

Q.187. Which Bhutan king visited India, as a Chief Guest at 56th Republic Day celebrations?
Ans. Jigme Singye Wangchuk.

Q.188. Which Chinese Prime Minister was in India on an official trip in April 2005?
Ans. Wen Jiabo.

Q.189. With what style of music would you associate Louis Armstrong?
Ans. Jazz.

Q.190. What kind of musical instrument is a piano?
Ans. Keyboard.

Q.191. Who is the author of the novel 'Pinjar'?
Ans. Amrita Pritam.

Q.192. To which instrument family does the double bass belong?
Ans. Violin.

Q.193. With which Indian sitarist did Yehudi Menuhin perform at the United Nations in 1967?
Ans. Ravi Shankar.

Q.194. Who won the best actor award at the 51st National Film Awards Ceremony?
Ans. Vikram.

Q.195. Which Indian composer is famous for his Telugu kirtanas and ragas?
Ans. Tyagaraja.

Q.196. Which section of Indian classical music is performed without the accompaniment of drums?
Ans. Alapa.

Q.197. Which form of Indian classical dance is indigenous to the state of Andhra Pradesh?
Ans. Kuchipudi.

Q.198. How many hand poses does the Bharatnatyam have?
Ans. Eleven.

Q.199. Which was Raj Kapoor's directorial debut film?
Ans. 'Aag'.

Q.200. Who won a National Award for film acting at the age of 80?
Ans. Premji.

Q.201. **Which was the first colour film to win best picture Oscar?**
Ans. Gone With the Wind.

Q.202. **Who is called the Shakespeare of Modern cinema?**
Ans. Orson Welles.

Q.203. **Who made fifteen films with one word titles in English?**
Ans. Alfred Hitchcock.

Q.204. **Which Indian writer was on the jury of 2000 Cannes festival?**
Ans. Arundhati Roy.

Q.205. **Who was the 'poet-turned-actor' in Priyadarshan's six-minute video 'Unko Yaad Karo'?**
Ans. A.B. Vajpayee.

Q.206. **What is Natya-Shastra a handbook of?**
Ans. Dramatic art.

Q.207. **Which form of Indian classical dance developed under the influence of both Hindu and Muslim cultures?**
Ans. Kathak.

Q.208. **Which form of Indian classical dance is traditionally enacted outdoors and goes on all night?**
Ans. Kathakali.

Q.209. **Which form of classical dance did Rabindranath Tagore popularize throughout the country?**
Ans. Manipuri.

Q.210. **Who was the first musician ever to receive a salary for composing music?**
Ans. Johann Sebastian Bach.

Q.211. **Which dance form are Birju Maharaj and Gopi Krishna renowned for?**
Ans. Kathak.

Q.212. **Which is a classical dance form of Kerala?**
Ans. Kathakali.

Q.213. **Which is a classical dance form of Andhra Pradesh?**
Ans. Kuchipudi.

Q.214. **Who directed the Bengali film 'Bhuvan Shome'?**
Ans. Mrinal Sen.

Q.215. **Who wrote the volume of poetry named "The Bird of Time"?**
Ans. Sarojini Naidu.

Q.216. **In 1913 Rabindranath Tagore won the Nobel Prize for which work of literature?**
Ans. Gitanjali.

Q.217. **Which musical instrument does Sharan Rani Mathur play?**
Ans. Sarod.

Q.218. **Which Indian state is associated with Baul singers?**
Ans. West Bengal.

Q.219. **Who was the first recipient of the Dada Saheb Phalke Prize for lifetime achievement in Indian cinema in 1970?**
Ans. Devika Rani.

Q.220. **Which Indian film maker established the Royal Bioscope Company?**
Ans. Hiralal Sen.

Q.221. **With which film was playback singing introduced in Indian cinema?**
Ans. 'Dhoop Chhaon'.

Q.222. **Which Indian film was adjudged the best foreign film of 1958 by the Hollywood Press Association?**
Ans. 'Do Aankhen Barah Haath'.

Q.223. **Which style of light classical music is ascribed to Nawab Wajid Ali Shah of Lucknow?**
Ans. Thumri.

Q.224. Which form of music did Amir Khusrow create?
Ans. Ghazal.

Q.225. Who directed the film 'Through the Eyes of a Painter'?
Ans. M.F.Husain.

Q.226. Who wrote the book 'Train to Pakistan'?
Ans. Khushwant Singh.

Q.227. Who is considered the father of the carnatic style of music?
Ans. Purandara Dasa.

Q.228. In which film did Nadia, the first Indian actress to perform all her stunts herself, make her debut?
Ans. Hunterwali.

Q.229. When was the first TV centre opened in India?
Ans. On August 15, 1959.

Q.230. Where is the highest TV tower in India located?
Ans. At Pitampura, Delhi.

Q.231. What is the title of the book about the Bhopal tragedy written by Lapierre and Moro?
Ans. It was five past midnight in Bhopal.

Q.232. The longest single-volume novel of the century is Vikram Seth's "A Suitable Boy". How many pages it has?
Ans. 1349.

Q.233. On whose novel is Girish Karnad's maiden film 'Samskara' based?
Ans. U.R. Ananthamurthy.

Q.234. In which film Richard Attenborough, who directed Gandhi, acted?
Ans. 'Shatranj Ke Khiladi'.

Q.235. Who is known as Grand old Man of Indian English Fiction?
Ans. R.K. Narayan.

Q.236. Which author's collection of short stories is titled 'Mansarovar'?
Ans. Prem Chand.

Q.237. With which instrument is Ustad Bismillah Khan associated?
Ans. Shehnai.

Q.238. What was Noddy's profession in the series by Enid Blyton?
Ans. Taxi Driver.

Q.239. Name the first book in JK Rowling's Harry Potter Saga.
Ans. Harry Potter and the Philosopher's Stone.

Q.240. What was the name of the flying island that Gulliver visited in his travels?
Ans. Laputa.

Q.241. For which ballerina did Uday Shankar create the dances 'Hindu Wedding' and 'Radha-Krishna'?
Ans. Anna Pavlova.

Q.242. Which nineteenth century Bengali playwright wrote Neel Darpan, attacking British Indigo planters?
Ans. Dina Bandhu Mitra.

Q.243. Which social activist and playwright was killed while performing a street play at Sahibabad in 1989?
Ans. Safdar Hashmi.

Q.244. Which Hindi film is based on Shakespeare's novel 'Macbeth'?
Ans. Maqbul.

Q.245. Name Ghalib's first compilation of Urdu verse that came out in 1821.
Ans. 'Nushka-i-Hamidia'.

Q.246. Which author created the 'Famous Five' series?
Ans. Enid Blyton.

Q.247. **Which Indian politician is the author of the book 'Meri Ikkyavan Kavitaayen'?**
Ans. Atal Bihari Vajpayee.

Q.248. **Which term often used in Indian classical music, comes from the Sanskrit word meaning 'colour' or 'passion'?**
Ans. Raga.

Q.249. **Which Indian dancer-choreographer created the ballet 'Lanka Dahan' using wooden masks from Sri Lanka?**
Ans. Uday Shankar.

Q.250. **Which is Shakespeare's longest play?**
Ans. Hamlet.

Q.251. **Who wrote the Harsha-Charita?**
Ans. Bana Bhatta.

Q.252. **Which ancient poem did Mahatma Gandhi refer to as his 'spiritual dictionary'?**
Ans. Bhagavad Gita.

Q.253. **In the world of cartoons, which group consisted of disciples of the mutant rat splinter?**
Ans. Teenage Mutant Ninja Turtles.

Q.254. **Which Punjabi poetess wrote 'Ajj Akhan Waris Shah Noo' while fleeing from Pakistan to India in 1947?**
Ans. Amrita Pritam.

Q.255. **Which was the first film directed by Kundan Shah?**
Ans. 'Jaane Bhi Do Yaaron'.

NATIONAL SYMBOLS

1. National Animal : Royal Bengal Tiger
2. National Bird : Peacock
3. National Flower : Lotus
4. National Game : Hockey

NATIONAL FLAG

The National Flag is a horizontal tricolour of deep saffron *(kesaria)* at the top, white in the middle and dark green at the bottom in equal proportion. The ratio of width of the flag to its length is two to three. In the centre of the white band is a navy-blue wheel which represents the *chakra*. Its design is that of the wheel which appears on the abacus of the Sarnath Lion Capital of Ashoka. Its diameter approximates to the width of the white band and it has 24 spokes. The design of the National Flag was adopted by the Constituent Assembly of India on 22 July 1947.

Apart from non-statutory instructions issued by the Government from time to time, display of the National Flag is governed by the provisions of the Emblems and Names (Prevention of Improper Use) Act, 1950 (No. 12 of 1950) and the Prevention of Insults to National Honour Act, 1971 (No. 69 of 1971). The Flag Code of India, 2002 is an attempt to bring together all such laws, conventions, practices and instructions for the guidance and benefit of all concerned.

The Flag Code of India, 2002, takes effect from 26 January 2002 and supersedes the 'Flag Code—Indias' as it existed. As per the provisions of the Flag Code of India, 2002, there shall be no restriction on the display of the National Flag by members of general public, private organizations, educational institutions, etc., except to the extent provided in the Emblems and Names (Prevention of Improper Use) Act, 1950 and the Prevention of Insults to National Honour Act, 1971 and any other law enacted on the subject.

STATE EMBLEM

The state emblem is an adaptation from the Sarnath Lion Capital of Ashoka. In the original, there are four lions, standing back to back, mounted on an abacus with a frieze carrying sculptures in high relief of an elephant, a galloping horse, a bull and a lion separated by intervening wheels over a bellshaped lotus. Carved out of a single block  of polished sandstone, the capital is crowned by the Wheel of the Law (*Dharma Chakra*).

In the state emblem, adopted by the Government of India on 26 January 1950, only three lions are visible, the fourth being hidden from view. The wheel appears in relief in the centre of the abacus with a bull on right and a horse on left and the outlines of other wheels on extreme right and left. The bell-shaped lotus has been omitted. The words *Satyameva Jayate* from *Mundaka Upanishad*, meaning 'Truth Alone Triumphs', are inscribed below.

NATIONAL ANTHEM

The song *Jana-gana-mana*, composed originally in Bengali by Rabindranath Tagore, was adopted in its Hindi version by the Constituent Assembly as the National Anthem of India on 24 January 1950. It was first sung on 27 December 1911 at the Calcutta Session of the Indian National Congress. The complete song consists of five stanzas. The first stanza contains the full version of the National Anthem:

जन गण मन अधिनायक जय हे

भारत भाग्य विधाता

पंजाब सिंधु गुजरात मराठा

द्रविड़ उत्कल वंग

विंध्य हिमाचल यमुना गंगा

उच्छल जलधि तरंग

तव शुभ नामे जागे

तव शुभ आशिष मांगे

गाहे तव जय गाथा

जन गण मंगल दायक जय हे

भारत भाग्य विधाता

जय हे जय हे जय हे

जय जय जय जय हे।

Playing time of the full version of the national anthem is approximately 52 seconds. A short version consisting of the first and last lines of the stanza (playing time approximately 20 seconds) is also played on certain occasions.

NATIONAL SONG

The song *Vande Mataram*, composed in Sanskrit by Bankimchandra Chatterji, was a source of inspiration to the people in their struggle for freedom. It has an equal status with *Jana-gana-mana*. The first political occasion when it was sung was the 1896 session of the Indian National Congress. The following is the text of its first stanza:

वंदे मातरम वंदे मातरम

सुजलाम सुफलाम मलयज शीतलाम

सस्य श्यामलाम मातरम वंदे मातरम

शुभ्र ज्योत्स्ना पुलकित यामिनिम

फुल्ल कुसुमित दुमदल शोभिनिम

सुहासिनिम सुमधुर भाषिणिम

सुखदाम वरदाम मातरम वंदे मातरम।

PRESIDENTS OF INDIA

Name	Tenure
Dr Rajendra Prasad (1884-1963)	26 January 1950-13 May 1962
Dr Sarvepalli Radhakrishnan (1888-1975)	13 May 1962-13 May 1967
Dr Zakir Husain (1897-1969)	13 May 1967-3 May 1969
Varahagiri Venkatagiri (1884-1980)	3 May 1969-20 July 1969 (Acting)
Justice Mohammad Hidayatullah (1905-1992)	20 July 1969-24 August 1969 (Acting)
Varahagiri Venkatagiri (1884-1980)	24 August 1969-24 August 1974
Fakhruddin Ali Ahmed (1905-1977)	24 August 1974-11 February 1977
B.D. Jatti (1913-2002)	11 Feb 1977-25 July 1977 (Acting)
Neelam Sanjiva Reddy (1913-1996)	25 July 1977-25 July 1982
Giani Zail Singh (1916-1994)	25 July 1982-25 July 1987
R Venkataraman (b-1910)	25 July 1987-25 July 1992
Dr Shanker Dayal Sharma (1918-1999)	25 July 1992-25 July 1997
K.R. Narayanan (b-1920)	25 July 1997-25 July 2002
Dr A.P.J. Abdul Kalam (b-1931)	25 July 2002-till date

VICE-PRESIDENTS OF INDIA

Name	Tenure
Dr Sarvepalli Radhakrishnan (1888-1975)	1952-1962
Dr Zakir Husain (1897-1969)	1962-1967
Varahagiri Venkatagiri (1884-1980)	1967-1969
Gopal Swarup Pathak (1896-1982)	1969-1974
B.D. Jatti (1913-2002)	1974-1979
Justice Mohammad Hidayatullah (1905-92)	1979-1984
R Venkataraman (b-1910)	1984-1987
Dr Shanker Dayal Sharma (1918-1999)	1987-1992
K.R. Narayanan (b-1920)	1992-1997
Krishan Kant (1927-2002)	1997-2002
Bhairon Singh Shekhawat (b-1923)	2002-till date

PRIME MINISTERS OF INDIA

Name	Tenure
Jawaharlal Nehru (1889-1964)	15 August 1947-27 May 1964
Gulzari Lal Nanda (1898-1997)	27 May 1964-9 June 1964 (Acting)
Lal Bahadur Shastri (1904-1966)	9 June 1964-11 January 1966
Gulzari Lal Nanda (1898-1997)	11 January 1966-24 January 1966 (Acting)
Indira Gandhi (1917-1984)	24 January 1966-24 March 1977
Morarji Desai (1896-1995)	24 March 1977-28 July 1979
Charan Singh (1902-1987)	28 July 1979-14 January 1980
Indira Gandhi (1917-1984)	14 January 1980-31 Oct 1984
Rajiv Gandhi (1944-1991)	31 October 1984-1 December 1989
Vishwanath Pratap Singh (b-1931)	2 Dec 1989-10 Nov 1990
Chandra Shekhar (b-1927)	10 November 1990-21 June 1991
P.V. Narasimha Rao (b-1921)	21 June 1991-16 May 1996
Atal Bihari Vajpayee (b-1926)	16 May 1996-01 June 1996
H.D. Deve Gowda (b-1933)	01 June 1996-21 April 1997
I.K. Gujral (b-1933)	21 April 1997-18 March 1998
Atal Bihari Vajpayee (b-1926)	19 March 1998-13 October 1999
Atal Bihari Vajpayee (b-1926)	13 October 1999-22 May 2004
Dr Manmohan Singh (b-1932)	22 May 2004-till date

CHIEF ELECTION COMMISSIONERS OF INDIA

Name	Tenure
Sukumar Sen	21 March 1950-19 December 1958
K.V.K. Sundaram	20 December 1958-30 Sept 1967
S.P. Sen Verma	1 October 1967-30 Sept 1972
Dr Nagendra Singh	1 October 1972-6 Feb 1973
T Swaminathan	7 Feb 1973-17 June 1977
S.L. Shakdhar	18 June 1977-17 June 1982
R.K. Trivedi	18 June 1982-31 Dec 1985
R.V.S. Peri Sastri	1 Jan 1986-25 Nov 1990
Smt. V.S. Rama Devi	26 Nov 1990-11 Dec 1990
T.N. Seshan	12 Dec 1990-11 Dec 1996
M.S. Gill	12 Dec 1996-13 June 2001
J.M. Lyngdoh	13 June 2001-8 Feb. 2004
T.S. Krishna Murthy	8 Feb 2004-15 May 2005
B.B. Tandon	16th May 2005-till date

GOVERNMENT OF NATIONAL CAPITAL TERRITORY OF DELHI

B.L. Joshi: L.G. of Delhi.

Sheila Dikshit: Chief Minister, Administrative Reforms, General Administration Department, Home, Law and Justice and Legislative Affairs, Public Relations, Services, Vigilance, Water, Higher Education, Training and Technical Education and all other subjects not allocated to any other minister.

A.K. Walia: Finance, Planning, PWD, Urban Development and Excise.

Raj Kumar Chauhan: Development, Revenue, Irrigation and Flood Control, Food and Civil Supplies, Environment and Forest, Welfare and SC/ST.

Haroon Yusuf: Transport and Power.

Yoganand Shastri: Health and Family Welfare and Social Welfare.

Mangat Ram Singhal: Industries, Labour, Employment, Elections and Land and Building.

Arvinder Singh Lovely: Education, Tourism, Art, Culture, Languages and Gurudwara Elections and Administration.

STATES AND UNION TERRITORIES OF INDIA

State	Capital
Andhra Pradesh	Hyderabad
Arunachal Pradesh	Itanagar
Assam	Dispur
Bihar	Patna
Goa	Panaji
Chhattisgarh	Raipur
Gujarat	Gandhinagar
Haryana	Chandigarh
Himachal Pradesh	Shimla
Jammu and Kashmir	Srinagar (summer)
	Jammu (winter)
Jharkand	Ranchi
Karnataka	Bangalore
Kerala	Thiruvananthapuram
Madhya Pradesh	Bhopal
Maharashtra	Mumbai
Manipur	Imphal
Meghalaya	Shillong
Mizoram	Aizawl
Nagaland	Kohima
Orissa	Bhubaneswar
Punjab	Chandigarh
Rajasthan	Jaipur
Sikkim	Gangtok
Tamil Nadu	Chennai
Tripura	Agartala
Uttaranchal	Dehra Dun
Uttar Pradesh	Lucknow
West Bengal	Kolkata
Union Territory	
Andaman and Nicobar Islands	Port Blair
Chandigarh	Chandigarh
Dadra and Nagar Haveli	Silvassa
Daman and Diu	Daman
Delhi	Delhi
Lakshadweep	Kavaratti
Pondicherry	Pondicherry

IMPORTANT NATIONAL DAYS

Date	Important Days
5th January	Army Day
23rd January	Netaji Subhash Chandra Bose's birth anniversary
26th January	Republic Day
30th January	Martyr's Day (Mahatma Gandhi's death anniversary)
24th February	Central Excise Day
28th February	National Science Day (On this day Nobel Laureate Dr C.V. Raman discovered the 'Raman effect')
18th March	Human Rights Day
13th April	Anniversary of Jallianwala Bagh Tragedy
14th April	Dr B.R. Ambedkar's birth anniversary
13th May	National Solidarity Day (Birth anniversary of Dr Fakhruddin Ali Ahmed)
21st May	Anti-terrorism Day (Death anniversary of Rajiv Gandhi)
22nd July	National Flag Adoption Day
9th August	Quit India Day
15th August	Independence Day
20th August	Sadbhavna Diwas (Birth anniversary of Rajiv Gandhi)
5th September	Teacher's Day (Birth anniversary of Dr Radhakrishnan)
2nd October	Gandhi Jayanti
8th October	Indian Air Force Day
31st October	National Rededication Day
14th November	Children's Day (Birth anniversary of Pandit Jawaharlal Nehru)
19th November	Citizen's Day
4th December	Indian Navy Day
7th December	Armed Forces Flag Day

IMPORTANT INTERNATIONAL DAYS

Date	Important Days
25th January	International Customs Day
8th March	International Women's Day
15th March	World Consumer Right's Day
21st March	World Disabled Day, World Forestry Day
23rd March	World Meteorological Day
7th April	World Health Day (WHO came into existence), No Smoking Day
12th April	World Day of Aviation and Cosmonautics
18th April	World Heritage Day
22nd April	Earth Day
1st May	International Labour Day
3rd May	International Press Freedom Day
17th May	World Telecommunication Day
24th May	Commonwealth Day
29th May	Mt Everest Day
31st May	World No Tobacco Day
1st June	World Population Day
5th June	World Environment Day
26 June	International Day Against Drug Abuse and Illicit Trafficking
27th June	World Diabetes Day
11th July	World Population Day
6th August	Hiroshima Day
8th September	International Literacy Day
15th September	World Peace Day
22nd September	Rose Day
27th September	World Tourism Day
2nd October	World Animal Day
5th October	World Habitat Day
9th October	World Postal Day
16th October	World Food Day
24th October	UNO Day
30th October	World Thrift Day
25th November	Meatless Day
1st December	World AIDS Day
10th December	Human Rights Day (Aniversary of the Human Rights Charter adoption by the UNO)

TIME PERIODS

Name	Period
Bicentennial	200 years
Biennial	2 years
Century	100 years
Decade	10 years
Centennial	every 100 yars
Decennial	every 10 years
Leap year	366 days
Millennium	1,000 years
Month	28-31 days
Olympiad	every 4 years
Quadrennial	every 4 years
Qudricentennial	every 400 years
Quincentennial	every 500 years
Quinquennial	every 5 years
Septennial	every 7 years
Sesquicentennial	every 150 years
Sexcentenary	600 years
Sexennil	every 6 years
Tercentenary	300 years
Triennial	every 3 years
Vicennial	every 20 years
Week	7 days
Year	365 days or 12 months or 52 weeks

ROMAN NUMERALS

I	one	XI	eleven	XXX	thirty
II	two	XII	twelve	XL	forty
III	three	XIII	thirteen	L	fifty
IV	four	XIV	fourteen	LX	sixty
V	five	XV	fifteen	LXX	seventy
VI	six	XVI	sixteen	LXXX	eighty
VII	seven	XVII	seventeen	XC	ninety
VIII	eight	XVIII	eighteen	C	one hundred
IX	nine	XIX	nineteen	CC	two hundred
X	ten	XX	twenty	D	five hundred
		XXI	twenty-one	M	one thousand

IMPORTANT DISCOVERIES

Discovery	Discoverer	Nationality	Year
Aluminium	Hans Christian Oerstedt	Denmark	1827
Atomic number	Henry Moseley	England	1913
Electron	Sir Joseph Thomson	England	1897
Hydrogen	Henry Cavandish	England	1766
Law of falling bodies	Galileo	Itlay	1590
Laws of gravitation & motion	Isaac Newton	England	1687
Magnesium	Sir Humphry Davy	England	1808
Neutron	James Chadwick	England	1932
Oxygen	Joesph Priestly	England	1772
	CW Scheele	Sweden	
Ozone	Christian Schonbein	Germany	1839
Proton	Ernest Rutherford	England	1919
Radioactivity	Antoine Henery Bacquerel	France	1896
Silicon	Jons Berzelius	Sweden	1824
Uranium	Martin Klaproth	Germany	1789
Uranus (Planet)	William Herschel	England	1781
X-rays	Willhelm Roentgen	Germany	1895

IMPORTANT INVENTIONS

Name of Invention	Inventor	Nationality	Year
Aeroplane	Orville and Wilbur Wrigth	U.S.A.	1903
Barometer	Evangelista Torrcelli	Itlay	1644
Bifocal Lens	Benjamin Franklin	U.S.A.	1780
Car (Petrol)	Karl Benz	Germany	1888
Diesel Engine	Rudolf Diesel	Germany	1895
Dynamo	Hypolite Pixii	France	1832
Helicopter	Etienne Oehnichen	France	1924
Laser	Charles H. Townes	U.S.A.	1960
Lift (Mechanical)	Elisha G. Otis	U.S.A.	1852
Motor Cycle	G. Daimler	Germany	1885
Printing Press	Johann Gutenberg	Germany	1455
Razor (safety)	King C. Gillette	U.S.A.	1895
Refrigerator	James Harrison & Alexander Catlin	U.S.A.	1850
Safety Pin	Walter Hunt	U.S.A.	1849
Slide Rule	William Oughtred	Britain	1621
Tank	Sir Ernest Swinton	Britain	1914
Telegraph	M. Lammond	France	1787
Telegraph Code	Samuel F.B. Morse	U.S.A.	1837
Telephone (perfected)	Alexander Graham Bell	U.S.A.	1876

MATHEMATICAL SYMBOLS

+	plus or positive
−	minus or negative
±	plus or minus, positive or negative
×	multiplied by
÷	divided by
=	equal to
≡	identically equal to
≠	not equal to
≢	not identically equal to
≈	approximately equal to
~	of the order of or similar to
>	greater than
<	less than
≯	not greater than
≮	not less than
≥	greater than or equal to
≤	less than or equal to
≫	much greater than
≪	much less than
√	Square root
∞	infinity
∝	proportional to
Σ	sum of
∏	product of
Δ	difference
∴	therefore
∠	angle
∥	parallel to
⊥	perpendicular to
:	is to

NOBEL PRIZE 2003

Nobel Prize 2003 were presented under the following categories:

Nobel Peace: Iranian laywer Shirin Ebadi.

Physics Nobel: Alexei A Abrikosov, a Russian and American citizen Vitali L, Ginzburg, a Russian and Anthony J. Legget, a British and U.S. citizen.

Chemistry Nobel: Peter Agre and Roderick Machinnon of America.

Economics Nobel: Robert F. Engle (America), Clive W.J. Granger (Britain).

Medicine Nobel: Paul Lauterbur (America), Peter Mansfield (Britain).

Literature Nobel: J.M. Coetzee (South Africa).

MAGSAYSAY AWARDS

The Magsaysay awards, instituted in 1957 to honour the memory of Ramon Magsaysay, the former President of Philippines, honour now six Asians each year who exemplify Magsaysay "greatness of spirit, integrity and devotion to liberty". The winners for 2003 are: **J.M. Lyngdoh (CEC of India),** for convincing validation of free and fair polls as the best hope of democracy in strifetorn India; **Dr Gayo Yaochi:** Public Service (a lady doctor of China); **Dr Shanta Sinha:** Community Leadership (Social Worker of India); **Shila Koronel:** Journalism, literature and communication (Journalist of Philippines); **Aniseto Guteres Lopes:** Emergent Leadership (a social worker of East Timor); **Tetsu Nakamura:** a Physicist of Japan; **Sayi Toyama:** An environmentalist of Japan (Peace and International Understanding).

NOBEL LAUREATES OF INDIAN ORIGIN

Amartya Sen (b-1933) Prof Amartya Sen is the recipient of the Nobel Prize for Economics for the year 1998, becoming the first Asian to have been honoured with the award. The santiniketan-born economist who is a pioneer in Welfare Economics has to his credit several books and papers on aspects of welfare and development. An economist with a difference, Prof. Sen is a humanist. He has distinguished himself with his outstanding writings on famine, poverty, democracy, gender and social issues. The 'impossibility theorem' suggested earlier by Kenneth Arrow states that it was not possible to aggregate individual choices into a satisfactory choice for society as a whole. Prof. Sen showed mathematically that societies could find ways to alleviate such a poor outcome.

Subramanian Chandrashekar (1910-1995): The Nobel Prize for Physics in 1983 was awarded to Dr S. Chandrashekar, an Indian-born astrophysicist. Educated in Presidency College, Chennai, Dr Chandrashekar happened to be the nephew of his Nobel forbear, Sir CV Raman. He later migrated to the United States where he authored several books on Astrophysics and Stellar Dynamics. He developed a theory on white dwarf stars which posts a limit of mass of dwarf stars known also an Chandrashekar Limit. His theory explains the final stages of stellar evolution.

Mother Teresa (1910-1997): The Nobel Peace Prize was awarded to Mother Teresa in 1979. Albanian parentage, Agnes Gonxha Bojaxhiu was born at Skopje, now in Yogoslavia. She joined the Irish order of the Sisters of Loretto at Dublin in 1928 and came to Kolkata in 1929 as a missionary, only to find the misery of the abandoned and the destitute. Concern for the poor and the sick prompted her to found a new congregation, Missionaries of Charity. Having become an Indian citizen, Mother Teresa served the cause of dying destitutes, lepers and drug addicts, through *Nirmal Hriday* (meaning Pure Heart), the main centre of her activity. Her selfless service and unique devotion, not only to helpless fellow-Indians but also to the cause of world peace, earned her and India the first Nobel Peace Prize.

Hargobind Khorana (b 1922): Hargobind Khorana was awarded the Nobel Prize for Medicine in 1968. Of Indian origin, Dr Khorana was born in Raipur, Punjab (now in Pakistan). He took his doctoral degree in Chemistry from Liverpool University and joined the University of Wisconsin as a Faculty Member in 1960. His major breakthrough in the field of Medicine—interpreting the genetic code and analyzing its function in protein synthesis—fetched him the Nobel Prize.

Chandrashekar Venkataraman (1888-1970): India's first Nobel Prize for Physics was claimed in 1930 by the renowned physicist Sir C.V. Raman. Born at Thiruvanaikkaval near Tiruchirapalli in Tamil Nadh, Raman studied at Presidency College, Chennai. Later, he served as Professor of Physics at Calcutta University. Recipient of many honours and awards, including the title of 'Sir', Sir C.V. Raman received the Nobel Prize for an important optics research, in which he discovered that diffused light contained rays of other wavelengths— what is now popularly known as Raman Effect. His theory discovered in 1928 explains the change in the frequency of light passing through a transparent medium.

Rabindranath Tagore (1861-1941): Rabindranath Tagore was the first Indian ever to receive a Nobel Prize. Popularly known as *Gurudev*, India's Poet Laureate Tagore was born on 7 May 1861 in Kolkata. He was awarded the Nobel Prize for Literature in recognition of his work *Geetanjali*, a collection of poems in 1913.

ABBREVIATIONS

S.No.	Abbreviations	Full-Form
1.	AAFI	Amateur Athletics Federation of India
2.	AC	Alternating Current; Ashok Chakra; Ante Christum (Before Christ)
3.	AD	Anno Domini (After Christ)
4.	ADB	Asian Development Bank
5.	ADF	Asian Development Fund
6.	AEC	Atomic Energy Commission
7.	AERB	Atomic Energy Regulation Board
8.	AF	Audio Frequency
9.	AFC	Asian Football Confederation
10.	AFTC	Asia Foundation for Thermonuclear Studies
11.	AG	Adjutant General; Accountant General; Attorney General
12.	AI	Air India; Artificial Intelligence
13.	AIADMK	All India Anna Dravida Munnetra Kazhagam
14.	AICC	All India Congress Committee
15.	AICS	All India Council of Sports
16.	AICTE	All India Council for Technical Education
17.	AID	Agency for International Development
18.	AIDS	Acquired Immune Deficiency Syndrome
19.	AIDWA	All India Democratic Women's Association
20.	AIFF	All India Football Federation
21.	AIIMS	All India Institute of Medical Sciences
22.	AIMA	All India Management Association
23.	AIR	All India Radio

24.	**AIU**	Association of Indian Universities
25.	**AIWHA**	All India Women Hockey Association
26.	**AM**	Ante Meridiem (before noon)
27.	**AMC**	Army Medical Corps
28.	**AMU**	Aligarh Muslim University; Asian Monetary Union
29.	**AP**	Andhra Pradesh; Associated Press
30.	**APPLE**	Ariane Passenger Payload Experiment
31.	**ASEAN**	Association of South East Asian Nations
32.	**ASI**	Archaeological Survey of India
33.	**ASLV**	Augmented Satellite Launch Vehicle
34.	**ASSOCHAM**	Associated Chamber of Commerce and Industry
35.	**AT & T**	American Telegraphic and Telephone Co. Ltd.
36.	**ATC**	Air Traffic Control
37.	**ATM**	Automatic Teller Machine
38.	**AVSM**	Ati Vishisht Seva Medal
39.	**B.Com**	Bachelor of Commerce
40.	**B.Ed**	Bachelor of Education
41.	**B.P.Ed**	Bachelor of Physical Education
42.	**B.Pharm**	Bachelor of Pharmacy
43.	**B.Sc**	Bachelor of Science
44.	**BAC**	Business Advisory Committee
45.	**BAI**	Badminton Association of India
46.	**BALCO**	Bharat Aluminium Company Ltd.
47.	**BARC**	Bhabha Atomic Research Centre
48.	**BBC**	British Broadcasting Corporation
49.	**BC**	Before Christ
50.	**BCCI**	Board of Control for Cricket in India; Bank of Credit and Commerce International
51.	**BHEL**	Bharat Heavy Electricals Ltd.
52.	**BHU**	Banaras Hindu University
53.	**BILT**	Ballarpur Industries Limited
54.	**BIS**	Bureau of Indian Standards; Bank of International Settlement
55.	**BITS**	Birla Institute of Technology and Sciences

56.	**BJP**	Bharatiya Janata Party
57.	**BMW**	Bayerische Motoren Warke AG
58.	**BP**	Blood Pressure
59.	**BPO**	Business Process Outsourcing
60.	**bps**	bytes per second
61.	**BRAI**	Broadcast Regulatory Authority of India
62.	**BRO**	Border Roads Organisation
63.	**BSE**	Bombay Stock Exchange
64.	**BSES**	Bombay Suburban Electricity Supply
65.	**BSF**	Border Security Force
66.	**BSI**	Botanical Survey of India
67.	**BSNL**	Bharat Sanchar Nigam Ltd.
68.	**BSP**	Bahujan Samaj Party
69.	**CA**	Chartered Accountant
70.	**CAS**	Chief of the Air Staff; Conditional Access System
71.	**CAT**	Computerised Arial Tomography; Central Administrative Tribural
72.	**CBI**	Central Bureau of Investigation
73.	**CBSE**	Central Board of Secondary Education
74.	**CBT**	Children's Book Trust
75.	**CCI**	Cricket Club of India; Cement Corporation of India
76.	**CDAC**	Centre for Development of Advanced Computing
77.	**CDMA**	Code Division Multiple Access
78.	**C-DOT**	Centre for Development of Telematics
79.	**CD-ROM**	Compact Disc-Read Only Memory
80.	**CEC**	Chief Election Commissioner; Chief Executive Councillor
81.	**CEO**	Chief Electoral Officer; Chief Executive Officer
82.	**CGF**	Commonwealth Games Federation
83.	**CGHS**	Central Government Health Scheme
84.	**CGI**	Common Gateway Interface
85.	**CHOGM**	Commonwealth Heads of Government Meeting
86.	**CHOGRM**	Commonwealth Heads of Government Regional Meeting

87.	**CIA**	Central Intelligence Agency (USA)
88.	**CID**	Criminal Investigation Department
89.	**CITU**	Centre of Indian Trade Unions
90.	**CM**	Chief Minister; Common Market
91.	**CMC**	Computer Maintenance Corporation
92.	**CMIE**	Centre for Monitoring Indian Economy
93.	**CMO**	Chief Medical Officer
94.	**CMP**	Common Minimum Programme
95.	**CNG**	Compressed Natural Gas
96.	**CNN**	Cable News Network
97.	**CO**	Commanding Officer
98.	**COD**	Cash on Delivery; Central Ordnance Depot
99.	**CPF**	Contributory Provident Fund
100.	**CPI**	Communist Party of India
101.	**CPI(M)**	Communist Party of India (Marxist)
102.	**CPMT**	Combined Pre-Medical Test
103.	**CPWD**	Central Public Works Department
104.	**CRPF**	Central Reserve Police Force
105.	**CRRI**	Central Road Research Institute
106.	**CRY**	Child Relief and You
107.	**CSIR**	Council of Scientific and Industrial Research
108.	**CST**	Central Sales Tax
109.	**CTBT**	Comprehensive Test Ban Treaty
110.	**CTV**	Colour Television
111.	**CV**	Curriculum Vitae
112.	**CVC**	Central Vigilance Commission
113.	**D Phil**	Doctor of Philosophy
114.	**DA**	Daily Allowance; Dearness Allowance
115.	**DAE**	Department of Atomic Energy
116.	**DC**	Direct Current; Deputy Commissioner
117.	**DD**	Doordarshan
118.	**DDA**	Delhi Development Authority
119.	**DDT**	Dichloro Diphenyl Trichloroethane (insecticide)
120.	**DG**	Director General; Dei Gratia (by the Grace of God)

121.	**DIG**	Deputy Inspector General
122.	**DM**	District Magistrate
123.	**DMK**	Dravida Munnetra Kazhagam
124.	**DMRC**	Delhi Metro Rail Corporation
125.	**DMRTS**	Delhi Metro Rapid Transport System
126.	**DNA**	Di-oxyribonucleic Acid (biological elements)
127.	**DOTS**	Directly Observed Treatment Short-course
128.	**DPT**	Diptheria, Pertussis and Tetanus (Vaccine)
129.	**DRDO**	Defence Research and Development Organisation
130.	**DST**	Department of Science and Technology
131.	**DTH**	Direct-to-Home
132.	**DVD**	Digital Versatile/Video Disc
133.	**ECG**	Electro Cardio Graph
134.	**EFTA**	European Free Trade Association
135.	**e.g.**	exempli gratia (for example)
136.	**EGP**	Exterior Gateway Protocol
137.	**ELBS**	English Language Book Society
138.	**E-mail**	Electronic Mailing
139.	**ENT**	Ear, Nose and Throat
140.	**EPABX**	Electronic Private-Automatic Branch Exchange
141.	**EPF**	Employees Provident Fund
142.	**ESMA**	Essential Services Maintenance Act
143.	**EVM**	Electronic Voting Machine
144.	**f.o.b.**	Free on board
145.	**FACTS**	Fingerprint Analysis and Criminal Tracing System
146.	**FAO**	Food and Agriculture Organisation (of United Nations)
147.	**FBI**	Federal Bureau of Investigation (of USA)
148.	**FCI**	Food Corporation of India
149.	**FDI**	Foreign Direct Investment
150.	**FERA**	Foreign Exchange Regulation Act
151.	**FICCI**	Federation of Indian Chambers of Commerce and Industry
152.	**FIEO**	Federation of Indian Exports Organisations

153.	**FIFA**	International Football Federation
154.	**FIH**	International Hockey Federation
155.	**FM**	Field Marshal; Frequency Modulation
156.	**FORE**	Foundation for Organisational Research and Education
157.	**FPS**	Fair Price Shop
158.	**FTP**	File Transfer Protocol
159.	**FTU**	Free Trade Union
160.	**GAIL**	Gas Authority of India Limited
161.	**GATE**	Graduate Aptitude Test in Engineering
162.	**GATT**	General Agreement on Tariffs and Trade
163.	**GDP**	Gross Domestic Product
164.	**GM**	General Manager; General Motors
165.	**GMAT**	Graduate Management Admission Test
166.	**GMT**	Greenwich Mean Time
167.	**GNP**	Gross National Product
168.	**Govt.**	Government
169.	**GPF**	General Provident Fund; Gandhi Peace Foundation
170.	**GPO**	General Post Office
171.	**GRAM**	Geo Reference Area Management
172.	**GSI**	Geological Survey of India
173.	**GSLV**	Geo-synchronous Satellite Launch Vehicle
174.	**HAL**	Hindustan Aeronautics Limited
175.	**HC**	House of Commons; High Court
176.	**HCF**	Highest Common Factor
177.	**HDFC**	Housing Development Finance Corporation
178.	**HDI**	Human Development Index
179.	**HMT**	Hindustan Machine Tools; Head Micro Telephone
180.	**HMV**	His Master's Voice
181.	**hp**	Horse power
182.	**HQ**	Headquarters
183.	**Hr**	Hour
184.	**HRD**	Human Resource Development

185.	**HT**	Hindustan Times
186.	**IAAF**	International Amateur Athletic Federation
187.	**IAF**	Indian Air Force
188.	**IAS**	Indian Administrative Service
189.	**ICAR**	Indian Council of Agricultural Research
190.	**ICC**	International Cricket Council
191.	**ICCR**	Indian Council for Cultural Relations
192.	**ICCW**	Indian Council of Child Welfare
193.	**ICDS**	Integrated Child Development Scheme
194.	**ICHR**	Indian Council of Historical Research
195.	**ICICI**	Industrial Credit and Investment Corporation of India
196.	**ICMR**	Indian Council of Medical Research
197.	**ICRC**	International Committee of Red Cross
198.	**ICSSR**	Indian Council of Social Sciences Research
199.	**ICWA**	Indian Council of World Affairs
200.	**IDA**	Indian Dairy Association
201.	**IDBI**	Industrial Development Bank of India
202.	**IFA**	Indian Football Association
203.	**IFS**	Indian Foreign Service; Indian Forest Service
204.	**IHF**	Indian Hockey Federation
205.	**IIIT**	Indian Institute of Information Technology
206.	**IIM**	Indian Institute of Management
207.	**IMF**	International Monetary Fund
208.	**INA**	Indian National Army; Iraqi News Agency
209.	**INSA**	Indian National Science Academy
210.	**INSAT**	Indian National Satellite
211.	**IOA**	Indian Olympic Association
212.	**IOC**	International Olympic Committee; Indian Oil Corporation
213.	**IPC**	Indian Penal Code
214.	**IPS**	Indian Police Service
215.	**IQ**	Intelligence Quotient
216.	**IR**	Information Retrieval
217.	**IRC**	International Red Cross

218.	**ISI**	Indian Statistical Institute
219.	**ISO**	International Organisation for Standardisation
220.	**ISRO**	Indian Space Research Organisation
221.	**IST**	Indian Standard Time
222.	**ITI**	Indian Telephone Industries; Industrial Training Institute
223.	**ITO**	Income Tax Officer; International Trade Organisation
224.	**ITPO**	Indian Trade Promotion Organisation
225.	**JNU**	Jawaharlal Nehru University
226.	**JRC**	Junior Red Cross
227.	**KG**	Kidergarten
228.	**Kph**	Kilometer per hour
229.	**KVS**	Kendriya Vidyalaya Sangathan
230.	**LAN**	Local Area Network
231.	**LASER**	Light Amplification by Stimulated Emission of Radiation
232.	**LBW**	Leg Before Wicket
233.	**LCD**	Liquid Crystal Display; Least Common Denominator
234.	**LCM**	Lowest Common Multiple
235.	**LIC**	Life Insurance Corporation
236.	**LLB**	Legum Baccalareous (Bachelor of Laws)
237.	**LLM**	Master of Laws
238.	**LoC**	Line of Control
239.	**MA**	Master of Arts
240.	**MAT**	Management Aptitude Test; Minimum Alternate Tax
241.	**MBA**	Master of Business Administration
242.	**MBBS**	Bachelor of Medicine and Bachelor of Surgery
243.	**MCA**	Monetary Compensatory Account; Master of Computer Application
244.	**MCC**	Marylebone Cricket Club; Missile Control Centre
245.	**MCD**	Municipal Corporation of Delhi
246.	**MCI**	Medical Council of India

247.	**MD**	Managing Director; Doctor of Medicine
248.	**M Ed**	Master of Education
249.	**MLA**	Member of Legislative Assembly; Money Laundering Act
250.	**MMS**	Multimedia Messaging Service
251.	**MNC**	Multinational Corporation
252.	**MO**	Money Order; Medical Officer
253.	**MOB**	Management by Objectives
254.	**MODEM**	Modulator Demodulator
255.	**MP**	Member of Parliament; Military Police; Madhya Pradesh
256.	**M Sc**	Master of Science
257.	**MSS**	Manuscripts
258.	**N & Q**	Notes and Queries
259.	**NA**	Not Applicable
260.	**NAFED**	National Agricultural Cooperative Marketing Federation of India Ltd.
261.	**NASA**	National Aeronautics and Space Administration
262.	**NASDAQ**	National Association of Securities Dealers Automated Quotation
263.	**NBT**	National Book Trust
264.	**NCERT**	National Council of Educational Research and Training
265.	**NCSC & ST**	National Commission for Scheduled Castes and Scheduled Tribes
266.	**NCTE**	National Council for Teachers Education
267.	**NDA**	National Defense Academy
268.	**NIEPA**	National Institute for Educational Planning and Administration
269.	**NIFT**	National Institute of Fashion Technology
270.	**NLTA**	National Lawn Tennis Association
271.	**NRI**	Non-Resident of India
272.	**NSCI**	National Sports Club of India
273.	**NSNIS**	Netaji Subhash National Institute of Sports
274.	**NSS**	National Service Scheme
275.	**ONGC**	Oil and Natural Gas Corporation

276.	**PAL**	Phase Alternative Line
277.	**PAN**	Permanent Account Number
278.	**PIN**	Postal Index Number
279.	**PM**	Prime Minister
280.	**PO**	Post Office; Postal Order
281.	**POW**	Prisoner of War
282.	**PPF**	Planet Protection Fund, Public Provident Fund
283.	**PRO**	Public Relation Officer
284.	**PSLV**	Polar Satellite Launch Vehicle
285.	**PT**	Physical Training
286.	**PTBT**	Partial Test Ban Treaty
287.	**PTI**	Press Trust of India
288.	**RADAR**	Radio Detecting and Ranging
289.	**RAW**	Research and Analysis Wing
290.	**RNI**	Registrar of Newspapers of India
291.	**RPM**	Revolutions Per Minute
292.	**SAARC**	South Asian Association for Regional Cooperation
293.	**SHO**	Station House Officer
294.	**SLV**	Satellite Launch Vehicle
295.	**SNIPES**	Society of National Institutes for Physical Education and Sports
296.	**SOS**	Save Our Souls
297.	**SSC**	Staff Selection Commission
298.	**STC**	State Trading Corporation
299.	**STD**	Subscriber Trunk Dialing (Telephone)
300.	**TA**	Travelling Allowance; Territorial Army
301.	**TDA**	Trade Development Authority
302.	**TELEX**	Teleprinter Exchange
303.	**TISCO**	Tata Iron and Steel Company
304.	**TOEFL**	Test of English as a Foreign Language
305.	**TQM**	Total Quality Management
306.	**TRAI**	Telecom Regulatory Authority of India
307.	**UNCSTD**	United Nations Conference on Science and Technology
308.	**UNDP**	United Nations Development Programme

309.	**UNESCO**	United Nations Educational Scientific and Cultural Organization
310.	**UNICEF**	United Nations International Children's Education Fund
311.	**UNO**	United Nations Organization
312.	**UPSC**	Union Public Service Commission
313.	**UTI**	Unit Trust of India
314.	**VAT**	Value Added Tax
315.	**VIP**	Very Important Person
316.	**VPP**	Value Payable Post
317.	**VRS**	Voluntary Retirement Scheme
318.	**WADA**	World Anti-Doping Agency
319.	**WB**	World Bank
320.	**WHO**	World Health Organisation
321.	**WMO**	World Meteorological Organisation
322.	**WTO**	World Trade Organization
323.	**WWF**	Worldwide Wrestling Federation
324.	**ZSI**	Zoological Survey of India

Chapter two

Reasoning
and Logic

Q.1. What will be the 4th letter from right if the first three letters of the word HUMBLE are written in reverse order respectively?

Ans. H.

Q.2. How many meaningful English words can be formed from the first, fifth, seventh and ninth letter of the word, PUNCTUATE using them in different sequence only once?

Ans. Three.

Q.3. How many such pairs of letters are there in the word ALPHABET each of which has as many letters between them as in the word as in the alphabet?

Ans. Two.

Q.4. The man introduced a woman as "her husband is the only son of my mother". How is the man related to the woman?

Ans. Husband.

Q.5. What will come in place of question mark (?) in the following series of letters based on English alphabet?
BDFEGI   HJL   KMO ?

Ans. NPR.

Q.6. The position of Raju is 13th from top and 21st from bottom. Total how many students are there in the class?

Ans. 36.

Q.7. How many such 7 are there in the following arrangement, each of which is immediately preceded by 1 and immediately followed by 3?
8327153746173716674217353718

Ans. Two.

Q.8. How is C related to Q if R, the only daughter of Q is married to C?

Ans. Son-in-law

Questions 9 to 13:Each of these questions consist of a question and two statements numbered I and II. You have to decide whether the data provided in the statement are sufficient to answer. Read both statement and give answers:

1. If data in statement I alone is sufficient to answer the question, while data in statement II alone is not sufficient to answer.

2. If data in statement II alone is sufficient to answer the question, while the data in statement I alone is not sufficient to answer.

3. If the data either in statement I alone or in statement II alone is sufficient.

4. If the data in both the statements I and II together are not sufficient.

5. If both the statement I and II together are necessary.

Q.9. How is Radha related to Shyam?
   I : Shyam's wife, Monica has only one son, Surya.
   II : Radha is Surya's only sister.

Ans. 5.

Q.10. What is the colour of a parrot in a code language?
   I : In the code language 'Black' means 'Blue', 'Blue' means 'Pink' and 'Pink' means 'Green'.
   II : 'Green' means 'Yellow', 'Yellow' means 'White' and 'White' means 'Orange'.

Ans. 2.

Q.11. On which date of the month was Shruti born in Feb 2005?
    I : Shruti was not born on an even date of the month.
    II : Shruti's birthday was a prime number.

Ans. 4.

Q.12. What does 'so' stand for in a code language?
    I: 'no so' means 'go away' in the code language.
    II: 'So po' means 'far away' in the same code language.

Ans. 5.

Q.13. What is Ram's position from the right end of the row of 20 students?
    I: Ram is sitting immediately right to Laxmi who is tenth from left.
    II: Rani is sitting 3 places to the right of Ram and is fourteenth from the left.

Ans. 3.

Q.14. A mixture of oil and water contains 35% of oil by weight. 25 grams of water is added to 100 gm of such a mixture. What percentage of oil by weight is there in the new 'mixture'?

Ans. 28%.

Q.15. Rosa can eat 32 rasogollas in one hour. Her sister Lila needs three hours to eat the same number. How much will they take to eat 32 rasogollas together?

Ans. 45 minutes.

Q.16. Which of the following numbers fits into the blank space marked with question mark?

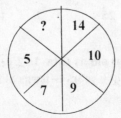

Ans. 18.

Q.17. **The point of concurrence of the three medians of a triangle is called what ?**

Ans. Centroid.

Q.18. **In the sequence of letters given below, which letters out of the given options fill the blanks to maintain the sequence?**
A, B, B, D, C, F, D, H, E, ..., ...

Ans. J,F.

Q.19. **HIV infection is necessary for having AIDS means what?**

Ans. If you have AIDS, you have HIV.

Q.20. **In one meal, Raja always eats one vegetarian dish out of Potato, Beans and Peas; one dish of cereals out of Rice and Chapati; and one non-vegetarian dish out of Chicken, Mutton and Fish. How many combination can he have of vegetarian cereal and non-vegetarian dishes?**

Ans. 18.

Q.21. **There are four vacant seats in a cinema hall. How many combination of four people can sit on those seats?**

Ans. 24.

Q.22. **π is a which type of number?**

Ans. Irrational number.

Q.23. **If the same functions are applied to reach the results in each of the 3 sets of numbers given below, then which number will replace question mark in the third set of numbers?**

21		5	28		13	16	2
	24			30			?
17		7	25		7	10	8

Ans. 30.

Q.24. **Anna is 5 times as old as Rita. In 2 years, Anna will be 3 times as old and in 6 years twice as old. How old Anna be in 7 years?**

Ans. 17 years.

Q.25. If 10 people can paint 60 houses in 120 days, then 5 people can paint 30 houses in how many days?

Ans. 120 days.

Q.26. Seth and Guru each have a collection of balls. Seth tells Guru that if he would give him four of his balls, then they would have same number of balls. But if Guru takes 4 balls, then Guru would have twice as many. How many balls does Seth have?

Ans. 20.

Q.27. If log x + log y = log (x + y) then y = ?

Ans. $y = \dfrac{x}{x-1}$.

Q.28. If the radius of a sphere is doubled, then its surface area is increased by how much %?

Ans. 300%.

Q.29. A trader marks his goods 20% above the cost price and allows a discount of 15%. His percentage gain will be what %?

Ans. 2%.

Q.30. What number of images can be produced if an object is placed in between two parallel mirrors facing towards each other?

Ans. Infinite.

Q.31. A baseball team has nine players. After winning a game, each player shook hands with each other just once. How many times did players shake hands?

Ans. 36.

Q.32. Replace?

84		81		88	
14	12	18	9	?	11

Ans. 16.

Q.33. A car company sold 150 cars in a special 6-day sale. Each day the company sold 6 more than previous day. How many cars were sold on the 6th day?

Ans. 40.

Q.34. $\dfrac{Sin\,70° + Cos\,40°}{Cos\,70° + Sin\,40°} = ?$

Ans. $\sqrt{3}$.

Q.35. $x = y^a$, $y = z^b$ and $z = x^c$, then what is the value of abc?

Ans. 1.

Q.36. If $\dfrac{a}{2b} = \dfrac{3}{2}$, then $\dfrac{2a+b}{a-2b}$ is equal to what?

Ans. 7.

Q.37. Replace ?
41 (28) 27
83 (?) 65

Ans. 36.

Q.38. What is the value of $\sqrt{0.121}$?

Ans. 0.348.

Replace (?) in Q. 39 and Q. 40

Q.39. Bird : Fly : : Snake : ?

Ans. Crawl.

Q.40. India : New Delhi : : Pakistan : (?)

Ans. Islamabad.

Q.41. 19 boys turn out of hockey. Of these 11 are wearing hockey shirts and 14 are wearing hockey pants. There are no boys without one or the other. The number of boys wearing full uniform is how many?

Ans. 6.

Q.42. What is the next number in the series?
0, 7, 26, 63, ...

Ans. 124.

Q.43. In a row of girls, Bina is 5th from the left and Priyanka is 6th from the right. When they exchanged their positions, then Bina becomes 13th from the left. What will be Priyanka's position from the right?

Ans. 14th.

Q.44. In a certain code 'BELIEF' is written as AFKKDI. How is SELDOM written in that code?

Ans. RFKFNP.

Q.45. In a certain code CERTAIN is coded as XVIGZRM, then how can MUNDANE be coded in that language?

Ans. NFMWZMV.

Q.46. The sum of a numerator and a denominator of a fraction is 11. If 1 is added to the numerator and 2 is subtracted from the denominator, then it becomes 2/3. What is the fraction?

Ans. 3/8.

Q.47. What is the value of $64 \div 8 \div 4 \div 2$?
Ans. 1.

Q.48. If $a : b = 2 : 3$, $b : c = 5 : 7$, then what is $a : b : c$?
Ans. 10:15:21.

Q.49. What is the perimeter of the given triangle?

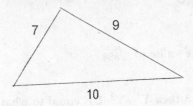

Ans. 26.

Q.50. The cost of 15 tables is equal to selling price of 20 tables. What is the percentage loss?

Ans. 25%.

Q.51. The perimeter of two similar triangles ABC and PQR is 45 feet and 30 feet respectively. If PQ = 12 feet, then what is the length of AB?

Ans. 18 feet.

Q.52. The numbers are in the ratio of 5 : 7 and its LCM is 315. What will be the product of these numbers?

Ans. 2835.

Q.53. X is twice as good a workman as Y. X finished a piece of work in 3 hours less than Y. In how many hours could they have finished that piece of work together?

Ans. 2 hours.

Q.54. What is the shortest distance between two intersecting lines?

Ans. 0.

Q.55. In the following figure, $\angle$ POS = 90°, $\angle$ ROQ = ?

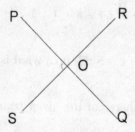

Ans. 90°.

Q.56. Find the value of $\sqrt{654}$.

Ans. 25.57.

Q.57. If Y = -3 then $Y^3 - Y^2 - 1$ is equal to what?

Ans. -37.

Q.58. A, B and C invested Rs. 26,000/-, Rs 34,000/- and Rs 10,000/- in a business. They earn a profit of Rs. 3500/-. What is B's share of profit?

Ans. Rs. 1700/-.

Q.59. What is the measure of ∠ABC if ABCD is a parallelogram, and the measure of ∠BAD is 88°?

Ans. 92°.

Q.60. If x : y = 3 : 4, y : z = 5 : 6 and z : w = 2 : 3, then x : w equals to what?

Ans. 5 : 12.

Q.61. A mixture of 40 litres of orange juice and water contains 10% of water. How much water should be added so that the quantity of water in the mixture becomes 20%?

Ans. 5 litres.

Q.62. Subtract –13 from 28 – 5 + 5.

Ans. 41.

Q.63. Add 7.007, 70.7 and 7.007

Ans. 84.714.

Q.64. At 3.40 hours, the hour-hand and minute-hand forms an angle of what?

Ans. 130°.

Q.65. If 14% of a number is 105, then find the number.

Ans. 750.

Q.66. What will be the length of the diagonal if the length is 12 cm and breadth is 5 cm?

Ans. 13 cm.

Q.67. What % of 54 is 45?

Ans. 83%.

Q.68. The value of
Cos 0° × Cos1° × Cos2° × Cos3° × ....Cos180° =?

Ans. 0.

Q.69. How many triangles are there in the figure?

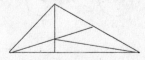

Ans. 11.

Q.70. **A man is performing yoga with his head down and legs up. His face is towards the west. In which direction will his left hand be?**

Ans. North.

Q.71. **At 12:30, the hour-hand of a clock faces North and the minute-hand faces South. At 1:45, hour-hand will be in which direction?**

Ans. North-West.

Q.72. **In a certain code MAN is written as SANM and WORD is written as SORDW. In that code how would SALE be written as?**

Ans. SALES.

Q.73. **If 123 means 'bright little boy', 145 means 'tall big boy', and 637 means 'beautiful little flower. Which digit represents 'bright'?**

Ans. 2.

Questions 74-78: In each of these questions, there are three circles with four numbers outside them. The number inside the circle is based on a definite pattern of four outside numbers. Find the missing (?) inside the third circle.

Q.74.

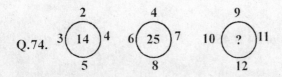

Ans. 42.

Q.75.

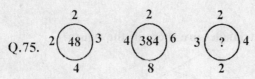

Ans. 48.

Q.76.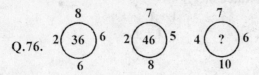

Ans. 46.

Q.77.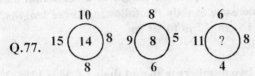

Ans. 6.

Q.78.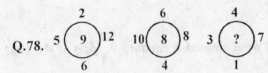

Ans. 5.

Q.79. Arrange the following in meaningful sentence:
(1) Shoulder (2) Wrist (3) Elbow (4) Palm (5) Finger

Ans. 5,4,2,3,1.

Q.80. If 25th August in a year is Thursday, then the Mondays in that month will be how many?

Ans. 5.

Q.81. 'E' is the son of 'A'. 'D' is the son of 'B'. 'E' is married to 'C', and 'C' is B's daughter. How is D related to E?

Ans. Brother-in-law.

Q.82. A cube, painted yellow on all faces, is cut into 27 small cubes of equal size. How many small cubes are painted on one face only?

Ans. 6.

Q.83. $\sqrt{2}$ is what number?

Ans. Irrational number.

Q.84. What is the value of $\dfrac{1\frac{1}{2}}{1+\dfrac{1}{1+\dfrac{1}{4}}}$?

Ans. 5/6.

Q.85. What is the greatest possible length of a scale that can be used to measure exactly the following three lengths? 3 m, 5 m to 10 cm, 12 m to 90 cm

Ans. 30 cm.

Q.86. The HCF of two numbers is 96 and their LCM is 1296. If one number is 864, then find the other number.

Ans. 144.

Q.87. $\dfrac{5}{12}$ part of what amount is equal to $3\dfrac{3}{4}$ part of Rs. 100?

Ans. Rs. 900.

Q.88. A drum of water is $\dfrac{3}{5}$ th full. When 38 litres are drawn from it, it is just $\dfrac{1}{8}$ th full. What is the total capacity of the drum?

Ans. 80 litres.

Q.89. If the cost of telephone calls in a town is 30 paise/call for first 100 calls, 25 paise per call for next 100 and 20 paise/calls for more than 200, then how many calls can be made in Rs. 50?

Ans. 180

Q.90. Find:

$$\frac{3+4\div2\times3}{4+3\times2\div3}=?$$

Ans. $\dfrac{3}{2}$.

Q.91. A reduction of Rs 2/- per kg in the price of sugar enables a man to purchase 4 kg more sugar now in Rs. 16/-. What was the original price of sugar?

Ans. Rs. 4/kg.

Q.92. 33% marks are required to pass an exam. A candidate who gets 210 marks, fails by 21 marks. What are the total marks for the examination?

Ans. 700.

Q.93. The ticket for admission to an exhibition was Rs 5 and it was later reduced by 20%. As a result the sale increased by 44%. What was the % increase in the number of visitors?

Ans. 80%.

Q.94. The average weight of 8 men is increased by 2 kg when one man of 50 kg is replaced by a new man. What is the weight of new man?

Ans. 66 kg.

Q.95. Nine men went to a hotel. 8 of them spent Rs 3 each over their meals and the ninth person spent Rs 2 more than the average expenditure of all the nine. What was the total money spent by all of them?

Ans. Rs. 27.50.

Q.96. The sum of present ages of A, B and C is 90 years. Six years ago, their ages were in the ratio of 1:2:3. What is the present age of C?

Ans. 42 years.

Q.97. The sum of salaries of 'A' and 'B' is Rs 2100. A spends 80% of his salary and B spends 70% of his salary. Their savings are in the ratio of 4:3. What is the salary of A?

Ans. Rs. 1400.

Q.98. Rs 1290 are divided between A, B and C, such that A's share is 1½ times that of B, and B's share is $1\frac{3}{4}$ times that of C. What is C's share?

Ans. Rs. 240.

Q.99. Five litres of water is added to a certain quantity of pure milk, which costs Rs 3/litre. If the mixture is sold at the same price of Rs. 3/litre, the profit is of 20%. What is the amount of pure milk in the mixture?

Ans. 25 litres.

Q.100. Fifteen men working 8 hours a day take 21 days to complete a work. How many days will be taken by 21 women to complete the same work, working 6 hours a day?

Ans. 30 days.

Q.101. 'A' can knit a pair of socks in 3 days. 'B' can knit the same pair in 9 days. If they are knitting together, then in how many days will they knit two pairs of socks?

Ans. 4½ days.

Q.102. Two electronic music systems are of Rs. 8000. One was sold at 40% profit and other was sold at 40% loss. If the selling price of both are the same, then what is the C.P. of both the systems?

Ans. Rs 3360.

Q.103. M. Price is 30% more than C.P. and 10% discount is allowed on M. Price. What will be the gain%?

Ans. 17%.

Q.104. A man has Rs 2000. Some portion of this amount, he lends @ 5% p.a. S.I. and the remaining portion of the same is lent at 4% p.a. S.I. He earns Rs 96 in a year. What amount was lent by him at 4%?

Ans. Rs. 1600.

Q.105. What sum will become Rs 496/- in 6 years @ 4% p.a.?
Ans. Rs. 400.

Q.106. Length, breadth and height of a room are 12 m, 9 m and 8 m respectively. What will be the length of diagonal?
Ans. 17 m.

Q.107. The difference between the circumference of a circle and its radius is 37 m. What is radius of the circle?
Ans. 7 m.

Q.108. A and B can cover 200 m race in 22 sec and 25 sec. respectively. When A finished the race then B is at what distance from finishing line?
Ans. 24 m.

Q.109. In a river, a man takes 3 hours in rowing 3 km upstream or 15 km downstream. What is the speed of current?
Ans. 2 km/hour.

Q.110. A 110 m long train is running @ 60 km/hr. How much time will it take to cover 240 m long platform?
Ans. 21 sec.

Q.111. A car covers a distance of 420 km at its normal speed. If the speed of car would have been 10 km/hr more, then it would have taken one hour less to cover the same distance. What was the speed of the car?
Ans. 60 km/hr.

Q.112. Amount doubles itself in 15 years. In how many years will it become 8 times?
Ans. 45 years.

Q.113. If a, a-2, 3a are in A.P., then what a is?
Ans. a = –2.

Q.114. How many committees of 5 members can be formed from 6 gentlemen and 4 ladies?
Ans. 252.

Q.115. Three identical dice are rolled. What is the probability that the same number will appear on each of them?

Ans. 1/36.

Q.116. A purse contains 5 silver and 2 gold coins. A coin is taken out of any purse. What is the probability that it is a silver coin?

Ans. 9/14.

Q.117. If w is the cubic root of the unit and n, a multiple of 3, then $1 + w^n + 2^{wn}$ is equal to what?

Ans. 3.

Q.118. If $4 \sin^{-1}x + \cos^{-1}x = p$ then x = ?

Ans. 1/3.

Q.119. The maximum value of Sin x + Cos x is what?

Ans. $\sqrt{2}$.

Q.120. What is the solution of the differential equation Cos x Cos y dx + Sin x sin y dy = 0 ?

Ans. Sin x = C cos y.

Q.121. What is the value of $\cos^{-1}(-1) - \sin^{-1}(1)$?

Ans. $3\pi/2$.

Q.122. If Sin A = Sin B and Cos A = Cos B, what is the value of A ?

Ans. $2n\pi + B$.

Q.123. The equation $x^2 + y^2 - 2xy - 1 = 0$ represents which type of curve?

Ans. Hyperbola.

Q.124. The content of lead in an ore is 25%. What is the amount of ore needed to get 80 kgs of lead ?

Ans. 320 kgs.

Q.125. A cubical block of 25 cm edge is melted to form new cubical blocks of 5 cm edge. How many new cubical blocks can be formed?
Ans. 125.

Q.126. If $(a-b) = 4$ and $ab = 2$, then $a^2 + b^2 = ?$
Ans. 12.

Q.127. If the area of a square is increased by 44%, then the increase in the side is by what %?
Ans. 20%.

Q.128. What is the sum of exterior angles of a triangle?
Ans. 360°.

Q.129. A circle and a square have same area. What is the ratio of side of the square to the radius of the circle?
Ans. $\sqrt{\pi}$: 1.

Q.130. 'A' can do a piece of work in 15 days, while 'B' can do in 10 days. 'B' worked at it for 8 days. 'A' can finish the remaining work in how many days?
Ans. 3 days.

Q.131. 16   24   36   54   81   121.5

14   (a)   (b)   (c)   (d)   (e)
What comes in place of (b)?
Ans. 31.5.

Q.132. 7   15   31   63   127   255
4   (a)   (b)   (c)   (d)   (e)
What will come in place of C?
Ans. 39.

Q.133. A tap can be filled completely with water in 8 hours. The water tank has a hole in it through which the water leaks out. The leakage will cause the water tank to get empty in 12 hours. How much time will it take to completely fill the tank with the hole?
Ans. Twenty-four hours.

Q.134. What value should come in place of (?)

$$48\sqrt{?} + 32\sqrt{?} = 32$$

Ans. 4/25 or 0.16.

Q.135. On the Children's Day, chocolates were to be equally distributed among 250 children. But on that day 75 children were absent. Thus each student got 3 chocolates extra. How many chocolates were distributed in all?

Ans. 1750 chocolates.

Q.136. Seven kg of sugar was available for Rs 84 last year. If this year nine kg of sugar is available for Rs 135, what is the % increase in price of sugar?

Ans. 25%.

Q.137. Mr Patkar earns Rs 10,000 p.m. Every year he spends 18% of his annual income on buying clothes. How much money does Mr Patkar spend every month on buying clothes?

Ans. Rs 1800.

Q.138. The price of 5 chairs and 3 tables is Rs 15015.20. What will be the price of 9 tables and 15 chairs?

Ans. Rs. 45,000.

Q.139. Three-fourth of two-third of five-seventh of a number is 15? What is half the number?

Ans. 21.

Q.140. Riya and Mita can independently complete a piece of work in 15 min. and 10 min. respectively. If they work together, then how much time will they take to complete the work?

Ans. 6 minutes.

Q.141. Kumar borrowed Rs 6500 from Devang on simple interest. After 4 years, Kumar paid back Devang Rs 2080 as interest, what was the rate of interest p.a.?

Ans. 8%.

Q.142. 50% of a number is 39 more than 35% of the same number. What is 115% of that number?

Ans. 299.

Q.143. The average age of 82 students and the class teacher is 18 years. The total age of only the students is 1450 years. What is the age of the class teacher?

Ans. 44 years.

Q.144. $3\sqrt{5} + \sqrt{125} = 17.88$. What will be the value of $\sqrt{80} + 6\sqrt{5}$?

Ans. 22.35.

Q.145. The average marks obtained by Amit in English and History is 95. The average marks obtained by him in English and Science is 87. What is the difference between marks obtained by him in History and Science?

Ans. 8.

Q.146. The total of the present ages of A and B together is 12 years more than the total of the present ages of B and C together. C is how many years younger than A?

Ans. 12 years.

Q.147. A student was asked to simplify the following:

$$7 \div \cfrac{3 - \cfrac{2}{3 - 1\frac{1}{2}}}{4 - 1\frac{1}{2}} - \frac{5}{7} \times \left[\frac{7}{10} + 1\frac{1}{5} \times \cfrac{3\frac{1}{3} - 2\frac{1}{2}}{2\frac{5}{21} - 2} \right] + \cfrac{\frac{3}{1.6} + \frac{5}{3.2}}{\frac{5}{4.8} + \frac{1}{9.6}}$$

His answer was $3\frac{1}{5}$. Find the percentage error:

Ans. 20%.

Q.148. Find the least multiple of 7 which when divided by 2,3,4,5 and 6, leaves the remainder 1,2,3,4 and 5 respectively?

Ans. 119.

Q.149. If $x = \sqrt{3/2}$, find $\dfrac{\sqrt{1+x} + \sqrt{1-x}}{\sqrt{1+x} - \sqrt{1-x}}$

Ans. $\sqrt{3}$.

Q.150. A man spends 80% of his income. With the increase in the cost of living, his expenditure increases by 37½% and his income increases by $16\dfrac{2}{3}$%. Find his present percent saving.

Ans. 5.71%.

Q.151. A principal sum of money is lent out at compound interest compounded annually at a rate of 20% p.a. for 2 years. It would give Rs. 2410 more if the interest is compounded half yearly. Find the principal sum.

Ans. Rs. 1,00,000.

Q.152. Average score of girls in class X is 73 and that of boys is 71. Average score in school is 71.8. Find the percentage of girls and boys in class X of the school.

Ans. Girls 40% and Boys 60%.

Q.153. What is the distance between the parallel lines 3x + 4y + 7 = 0 and 3x + 4y − 9 = 0 ?

Ans. 12/5.

Q.154. What is the value of $(8)^{1/3}$?

Ans. 2.

Q.155. A card is drawn from a pack of cards. Find the probability that the card will be queen or a heart.

Ans. 4/3.

Q.156. What is the maximum area of a square inside a circle?

Ans. $2a^2$.

Q.157. The multiplication inverse of a number is the number itself. Then what is its initial value?

Ans. −1.

Q.158. An even number of arithmetic means are inserted between two numbers whose sum is 13/6. If the sum of means exceeds their number by 1, what is the number of means?

Ans. 6.

Q.159. What is the coefficient of x^{10} in the expansion of $(1 + x + x^2 + x^3 + x^4)^{-2}$?

Ans. 3.

Q.160. What is the sum of the coefficients in the expansion of $(5x - 4y)^{100}$?

Ans. 1.

Q.161. A polygon has 54 diagonals. How many sides does it have?

Ans. 12.

Q.162. A team consists of three men, three women and three children. They have to stand in a line such that the men stand together, women stand together and children stand together. In how many different ways can this be done?

Ans. 1296.

Q.163. How many matrices of different order can be formed out of 36 elements (using all the elements at a time)?

Ans. 9.

Q.164. If the cost of 2 books and 3 pens is Rs. 120, and the cost of 5 books and 2 pens is Rs. 190, what is the cost of 8 books and 9 pens?

Ans. Rs. 420.

Q.165. The ratio of the sides of a triangle ABC is $1 : \sqrt{3} : 2$. What is the ratio A: B: C?

Ans. $1 : 2 : 3$.

Q.166. Three distinct numbers are selected from first 100 natural numbers. What is the probability that all the three numbers are divisible by 2 and 3?

Ans. $\dfrac{4}{1155}$.

Q.167. 6 boys and 5 girls are sitting around a round table. If no two girls sit together, then total ways of sitting are what?

Ans. $\lfloor 5 \ \lfloor 4 .$

Q.168. Argument of $-1 - i \sqrt{3}$ is what?

Ans. $\pi/3$.

Q.169. How many numbers between 8 to 101 are exactly divisible by 10 but not 5?

Ans. None.

Q.170. The rate of change of the volume of a sphere with respect to its surface area when its radius is 2 units is what?

Ans. 1.

Q.171. Out of 9 MPs and 5 ministers, a committee of 10 members is to be constituted. In how many can the committee be formed so as to include at least one minister?

Ans. 1001.

Q.172. If the 7th term of an Harmonic Progression is 3/11 and the 11th term is 3/17, then the 19th term is equal to what?

Ans. $\dfrac{3}{29} .$

Q.173. The number 110011001 in binary system can be expressed in decimal system as what?

Ans. 409.

Q.174. Anand plays with Karpov 3 games of chess. The probability that he wins a game is 0.5, loses with probability 0.3, and ties with probability 0.2. If he plays 3 games, then what is the probability that he wins at least two games?

Ans. 0.5.

Q.175. (0,0) is a vertex of a square and $5x - 12y + 26 = 0$ is the equations of one of its sides. What is the area of the square?

Ans. 4 sq. units.

Q.176. In a certain code the word KING is coded as 8,6,11,4; following the same code the word MONEY would be written as what?

Ans. 10,12,11, 2, 22.

Q.177. A pair of dice is rolled again and again till a total of 5 or 7 is obtained. What is the chance that a total of 5 comes before a total of 7?

Ans. 2/5.

Q.178. If A can do 1/4 of a work in 3 days and B can do 1/6 of the same work in 4 days, how much will A get if both work together and get a remuneration of Rs. 180 in all?

Ans. Rs 120.

Q.179. The power of the origin w.r.t. the circle $x^2 + y^2 - 6x + 8y - 16 = 0$ is what?

Ans. -16.

Q.180. The number of 7 digit number which can be formed using the digits 1, 2, 3, 2, 3, 3, 4 is what?

Ans. 420.

Q.181. If $\cos 20° = K$ and $\cos x = 2K^2 - 1$, then what are the possible values of x between 0° and 360°?

Ans. 40° and 320°.

Q.182. 12 more than 30 percent of a number is one-half the number. Find the number.

Ans. 60.

Q.183. What is the area of the region bounded by $y = |x-1|$ and $y = 1$?

Ans. 1.

Q.184. A light rod is acted on by three parallel forces P, Q, R acting at three points 2 cm, 8 cm and 6 cm respectively from one end. If the rod is in equilibrium, then P : Q : R is in which ratio?

Ans. 1:2:3.

Q.185. If the angles of a triangle are 30° and 45° and the included side is ($\sqrt{3}$ + 1) cm, then what is the area of the triangle?

Ans. $\dfrac{(\sqrt{3}+1)}{2}$ sq cm.

Q.186. If a, b, c are in harmonic progression, then what is the value of

$$\frac{b+a}{b-a}+\frac{b+c}{b-c}?$$

Ans. 2.

Q.187. What is the minimum distance between the parabolas $y^2 - 4x - 8y + 40 = 0$ and $x^2 - 8x - 4y + 40 = 0$?

Ans. $\sqrt{2}$.

Q.188. If A and B are two matrices such that AB = B and BA = A, what is then $A^2 + B^2$ equal to?

Ans. A + B.

Q.189. What are the number of ways to select 6 people out of 6 married couples in which exactly one couple is present?

Ans. 480.

Q.190. If points (5, 5), (10, K), (–5, 1) are collinear, then what is K equal to?

Ans. + 7.

Q.191. A sphere of radius r is divided into four identical parts. Find the total surface area of one part.

Ans. $2\pi r^2$ sq unit.

Q.192. What is the area of the curve $x^2 + y^2 = 2ax$?
Ans. πa^2.

Q.193. What is the area bounded by the angle bisector of the lines $x^2 - y^2 + 2y = 1$ and the line $x + y = 3$?
Ans. 2.

Q.194. The three angles A, B and C of a triangle ABC are in AP and $c^2 = a^2 + b^2$. If C = 50 metres, then what is the area of the triangle in square metres?
Ans. $\dfrac{625\sqrt{3}}{2}$.

Q.195. What is the sum of numbers lying between 107 and 253, which are divisible by 5?
Ans. 5220.

Q.196. If $\sin Q = \dfrac{24}{25}$ and $0° \angle Q \angle 90°$, then what is the value of $\sin\left(\dfrac{Q}{2}\right)$.
Ans. 3/5.

Q.197. What is the area of the triangle whose vertices are (0, 0, 0), (3, 4, 0) and (3, 4, 6)?
Ans. 15 square units.

Q.198. What is the derivative of $|x - 1| + |x - 4|$ at x = 3?
Ans. 0.

Q.199. ABC is a triangle and AD is the median. If the coordinates of A are (4, 7, –8) and the coordinates of centroid of the triangle ABC are (1, 1, 1), what are the coordinates of D?
Ans. $\left(-\dfrac{1}{2}, -2, \dfrac{11}{2}\right)$.

Q.200. Three dices are rolled. What is the probability of getting different faces?

Ans. 5/9.

Q.201. How many arrangements can be made out of the letters of the word MOTHER taken four at a time so that each arrangement contains the letter M?

Ans. 60.

Q.202. If the correlation coefficient between x and y is 0.7, what is the correlation coefficient between $U = 4x = 3$ and $V = \left(\dfrac{3y - 4}{2}\right)$?

Ans. 0.7.

Q.203. If w is a complex cube root of a unity and $1 + w^n + w^{2n} = 0$, what is the value of n?

Ans. 5.

Q.204. What is the variance of the first n natural numbers?

Ans. $\dfrac{n^2 - 1}{12}$.

Q.205. How much water must be added to one gallon of 8% saline solution to get a 2% saline solution?

Ans. 3 gallons.

Q.206. A lift is rising upwards with a uniform acceleration of 4.9 m/sec^2. A body of mass 20 kg is placed on a weighing machine in the lift. What will the weighing machine read?

Ans. 30 kg wt.

Q.207. What is the digit in the unit position of the integer $1! + 2! + 3! + 4! + \ldots\ldots + 98!$?

Ans. 4.

Q.208. If x = 1/5, the value of cos $(\cos^{-1} x + 2 \sin^{-1} x)$ is what?

Ans. $\sqrt{\dfrac{24}{25}}$

Q.209. The base of a rectangle is seven times the height. If the perimeter is 32 metres, what is the area?

Ans. 28 m^2.

Q.210. Let x be the number of times heads occur in n tosses of a fair coin. If P (x = 4), P (x = 5) and P (x = 6) are in Arithmetic Progression what is the value of n?

Ans. 7, 14.

Q.211. When 10 is subtracted from all the observations, the mean is reduced to 60% of its value. If 5 is added to all the observations, then what will be the mean?

Ans. 60.

Q.212. There are 10 men in a group and each one gives gift to others, then what is the total number of gifts received?

Ans. 90.

Q.213. In a joint family, an old farmer has four sons. Among four sons, each son has two sons and two daughters. The old farmer and her daughters-in-law are also in the family. How many members are in the family?

Ans. 25.

Q.214. If the 6th term in the expansion of the binomial $[1/x^{(8/3)} + x^2 \log x]^8$ is 5600 then what is x equal to?

Ans. 10.

Q.215. The number of integral values of a for which the equation cos 2x + a sin x = 2a – 7 possesses a solution is what?

Ans. 5.

Q.216. For any real Q, the maximum value $\cos^2$ (cos Q) + $\sin^2$ (sin Q) is what?

Ans. 1.

Q.217. What is the number of distinct normals drawn to the parabola $y^2 = 4x$ passing through the point $(14, -16)$?

Ans. 3.

Q.218. The sum of a number and its reciprocal in 10/3, find the numbers.

Ans. 3 or 1/3.

Q.219. What is the probability that a leap year selected at random will contain 53 Fridays?

Ans. 2/7.

Q.220. The LCM and HCF of two polymonials $p(x)$ and $q(x)$ are $2(x^4 - 1)$ and $(x + 1)(x^2 + 1)$ respectively. If $p(x) = x^3 + x^2 + x + 1$, find $q(x)$.

Ans. $q(x) = \pm (2x^4 - 2)$.

Q.221. Two poles of heights 6 m and 11 m stand vertically on a plane ground. If the distance between their feet is 12 m, find the distance between their tops.

Ans. 13 m.

Q.222. The sum of the infinite series $\text{Cot}^{-1} 2 + \text{Cot}^{-1} 8 + \cot^{-1} 18 + \cot^{-1} 32 + ...$ is equal to what?

Ans. $\pi/4$.

Q.223. The number of solutions of $\tan(5\pi \cos \alpha) = \cot(5\pi \sin \alpha)$ for α in $(0, 2\pi)$ is what?

Ans. 14.

Q.224. What is the number of solution of the equation $\cos(\pi\sqrt{x-4}) \cos(\pi\sqrt{\chi}) = 1$.

Ans. One.

Q.225. How many number of six digit numbers that can be formed from the digits 1, 2, 3, 4, 5 and 780 that digits do not repeat and the terminal digits are even?

Ans. 720.

Q.226. The number of solutions of the equation $2 \tan x + x =$ $\dfrac{12\pi}{5}$ in the interval $[\,0, 2p\,]$ is what?

Ans. 2.

Q.227. The absolute value of difference of maximum and minimum values of amp (z), where $|\,z - 5\,i\,| \leq 3$, is equal to what?

Ans. $\pi - 2 \cos^{-1}\left(\dfrac{3}{5}\right)$.

Q.228. What is number of three-digit numbers of the form xyz with $x > 1$ and digits are not repeated.

Ans. 576.

Q.229. There are 4 letters and 4 addressed envelopes. Find the probability that all the letters are not despatched in right envelopes.

Ans. 3/8.

Q.230. 19 more than a certain number is 63. What is the number?

Ans. 44.

Q.231. Which element is the third to the right of the thirteenth element from the right end?

Ans. M.

Q.232. If A is one year older than C, the number of logically possible orderings of all six cousins by increasing age is what?

Ans. 2.

Q.233. How many squares are there in a chess board?

Ans. 64.

Q.234. In a row of girls, Bina is 5th from the left and Priyanka is 6th from the right. When they exchange their positions, then Bina becomes 13th from the left. What will be Priyanka's position from the right?

Ans. 14th.

Q.235. A man is performing yoga with his head down and legs up. His face is towards the west. In which direction will his left hand be?

Ans. North.

Q.236. If the 25th of August in a year is Thursday, then what is the number of Mondays in that month?

Ans. 5 (1st, 8th, 15th, 22nd and 29th).

Q.237. 'E' is the son of 'A'. 'D' is the son of 'B'. 'E' is married to 'C', and 'C' is 'B's daughter. How is 'D' related to 'E'?

Ans. Brother-in-law.

Q.238. In a certain code, MAN is written as SANM and WORD is written as SORDW. In that code, how would SALE be written.

Ans. SALES.

Q.239. The next number in the series 0, 7, 26, 63 is what?

Ans. 124.

Explanation: [The terms of the given series are 1^3-1, 2^3-1, 3^3-1, 4^3-1, 5^3-1].

Q.240. The position of Raju is 13th from top and 21st from bottom. Total how many students are there in the class?

Ans. 33.

Q.241. How is C related to Q if R, the only daughter of Q, is married to C?

Ans. Son-in-law.

Q.242. Bird : Fly :: Snake:?

Ans. Crawl.

Q.243.

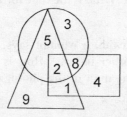

Find out the number that lies inside all the figures.

Ans. 2.

Q.244.

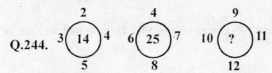

Find the ?

Ans. 42.

Q.245. "Furniture" is related to "Table" in the same way as "Stationery" is related to what?

Ans. Pencil.

Q.246. How many 3's are there in the following sequence which are neither preceded by 6 nor immediately followed by 9? 9 3 6 6 3 9 5 9 3 7 8 9 1 6 3 9 6 3 9.

Ans. Two.

Q.247. What will come in place of the question mark (?) in the following sequence?
DMU, EOT, FQS, (?)

Ans. GSR.

Q.248. If "BSTED" is written as "CRUDE", then "MOIST" will be written as what?

Ans. NNJRU.

Q.249. If 20–2 = 20, 25–4 = 50, 30 – 8 = 120, then 24–6=?.

Ans. 72.

Q.250. According to a military code, SYSTEM is SYSMET, and NEARER is AENRER. What is the code for FRACTION?

Ans. CARFNOIT.

Q.251. Pointing to a photograph, a woman says, "This man's son's sister in my mother-in-law." How is the woman's husband related to the man in the photograph?

Ans. Grandfather.

Q.252. Some numbers are written in the following codes:
1863
2094
57
In this code 195 is written as 307. How is 845 written in this code?

Ans. 627.

Q.253. Insert the proper suffix, which is common to all:
LAND
LIGHT
WATER (. . .)
PIT

Ans. FALL.

Q.254. ABDG, CDFI, EFHK, ?

Ans. GHJM.

Q.255. I go 10 metres to the east, then I turn left and go 5 metres, I turn left again and go 10 metres and then again I turn left and go 10 metres. In which direction am I from the starting point?

Ans. South.

Q.256. A cube painted blue on all the faces is cut into 125 cubes of equal sizes. How many cubes are not painted on any face?

Ans. 54.

Q.257. "Needle" is related to "Thread" in the same way as "Pen" is related to what?

Ans. Ink.

Q.258. The code for certain letters are indicated in the following words. BRAIN – 12345, GRADE – 72308, DRAIN - 02345, STATE—78388. What is the code for 'D'?

Ans. 0.

Q.259. Guilt : Past as Hope :?

Ans. Future.

Q.260. How many pairs of letters are there in the word BUCKET which have as many letters between them in the word as in the alphabet?

Ans. Four.

Q.261. When I was born, my mother was 23 years of age. After 6 years, when my sister was born, my father was 34 years of age. What is the difference between the ages of my parents?

Ans. 5 years.

Q.262. Vijay says, "Viju's mother is the only daughter of my mother". How is Vijay related to Viju?

Ans. Uncle.

Q.263. In a certain code FICTITIOUS is written as IFTCTIOISU. How is POSTPONE written in that code?

Ans. OPTSOPEN.

Q.264. In a certain code language 'pul tir fin' means 'good sweet fruit', 'tie dip sig' means 'beautiful red rose', 'sig lon fin' means 'rose and fruit'. In that language, what would stand for 'sweet'?

Ans. tir.

Q.265. If the word TERMINATION is coded as 12345671586, what should be the code for the word MOTION?

Ans. 481586.

Q.266. A group of 1200 persons consisting of captains and soldiers is travelling in a train. If for every 15 soldiers there is one captain, then what is the number of captains in the group?

Ans. 75.

Q.267. 3, 6, 18, 9, 18, 54, 27, 54, 162 (?)
Ans. 81.

Q.268. Picture : Frame :: Diamond : (?)
Ans. Setting.

Q.269. Fish : Bird :: Submarine: (?)
Ans. Aeroplane.

Q.270. Director : Movie :: (?) : Dance
Ans. Choreographer.

Q.271. Individual : Group :: Island : (?)
Ans. Archipelago.

Q.272. Lift : Elevator :: Petrol : (?)
Ans. Gasoline.

Directions: Read carefully the number letter series given below and answer the question from 273 to 277 based on the series.
D6 FAC L3 MJG1ZDYRU2EHIKNP4OQ

Q.273. If every alternative position is dropped starting from D, which will be the 5th to the right of the twelfth from left?
Ans. B.

Q.274. What will come in place of (?) in the series given below?
FAC. MJG BYR ?
Ans. EHI.

Q.275. Which of the following will be the 4th to the left of 10th position from your right?
Ans. M.

Q.276. If it is possible to make any meaningful word from the combination of 4th, 8th, 18th and 22nd letter in series, what will be the first letter of that word?
Ans. P.

Q.277. If every third letter starting from your right denotes the days of week starting from Monday, which will denote Wednesday?

Ans. E.

Q.278. In a certain code MADRAS is written as ODHWGZ. How DELHI is written in that code?

Ans. FHPMN.

Q.279. How many 9's are there in the following sequence which are immediately followed by 5 but not immediately proceeded by 4?
9953495329578149563499549275954954995

Ans. Five.

Q.280. In a queue Ashok is 6th from left and Ramesh is 10th from right. If there are 8 boys between Ramesh and Ashok, how many boys are there in a queue?

Ans. 24.

Q.281. How many number of pairs of letter are there in the word PRODIGAL having same number of words between them as in alphabets?

Ans. Three.

Q.282. Three of the given four are alike in certain way and thus form a group. Which is the one that does not belong to the group?

December September January March.

Ans. September.

Q.283. Clock : Time : : ? : Temperature.

Ans. Thermometer.

Q.284. Book : Author : : Statue : ?

Ans. Sculptor.

Q.285. Raghav is father of Amar and Vijaya is mother of Gopal. The brother of Aman and Madan is Gopal. What is the relation of Vijaya and Madan?

Ans. Mother.

Q.286. If CONSTITUTION is coded as COSNTIUTTINO. How DISTRIBUTION is coded?

Ans. DITSIRUBTINO.

Q.287. Find the minimum number of colours required to paint all side of dice so that any two adjacent faces do not have the same colour.

Ans. Three.

Q.288. How many triangles does the figure has?

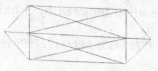

Ans. 28.

Q.289. In a certain code language 'Tun Min Sam' means 'Sugar is Bad', 'Sam Cot Cim' means 'Salt is Best' and 'Yah, Ton Min Top' means 'Do Away Best Bad'. Which of the following means 'Sugar' in that language?

Ans. Tun.

Q.290. Ramesh went to movie 11 days ago. He goes to movie only on Tuesday. What day of the week will be the day after tomorrow?

Ans. Monday.

Q.291. Ajay works more than Ramesh. Shyam works as much as Mohan. Pawan works less than Shyam. Ramesh works more than Shyam. Who works the most of all?

Ans. Ajay.

Q.292. In a certain code TRIPPLE is coded as SQHOOKD, how DISPOSE can be coded?

Ans. EJTPTFD.

Q.293. Out of the given four pairs of number one pair is different from others. Find that pair?
[13, 39], [21, 15], [24, 48], [81, 63]

Ans. [24, 48].

Q.294. B, D, F, H, (?).
Ans. J.

Q.295. A, Z, C, X, E, (?).
Ans. V.

Q.296. ZUA, XOC, VIE, TEG, (?).
Ans. RAI.

Q.297. 3, F, 9, L, 15, (?).
Ans. R.

Q.298. J, M, (?), V.
Ans. Q.

Q.299. AB, DEF, HIJK, (?), STUVWX.
Ans. MNOPQ.

Q.300. nsi, org, pqe, qpc, (?).
Ans. roa.

Q.301. EXTRAVAGANZA, TRAVAGANZA, TRAVAGANZ, (?).
Ans. AVAGANZ.

Q.302. AUY, DVW, GWU, JXS, (?).
Ans. MYQ.

Q.303. B, E, I, N, T, (?).
Ans. A.

Q.304. MN, LO, KP, JQ, IR, (?).
Ans. HS.

Q.305. XDA, WED, VFG, UGJ, THM, (?)
Ans. SIP.

Q.306. BXJ, ETL, HPN, KLP, (?).
Ans. NHR.

Q.307. DEF, HIJ, MNO, (?).
Ans. STU.

> Find the missing letters from Questions 308 to 321

Q.308. __bca___ca___ca___
Ans. abbc.

Q.309. ___m___1___1___ml___m___
Ans. 11m111.

Q.310. ab___c___c___a___ab___a___cc
Ans. cbacbb.

Q.311. a___c___ba___ca___cb
Ans. bcba.

Q.312. a___bbabb___ab___b
Ans. bbb.

Q.313. a___ ___b a___b___aa___b
Ans. ababb.

Q.314. cab___a___c___bc___bc___b ___ab
Ans. cbaaac.

Q.315. a___b___aabb___a___ ___a___bb
Ans. ababba.

Q.316. cccbb___aa___cc___bbbaa___c
Ans. baca.

Q.317. b___b___bb___ ___bab___bb___b
Ans. ababba.

Q.318. ccb___c___bbc___b___cc___ ___ccbb
Ans. bccbbb.

Q.319. bcaa___bcaab___bc___ab___b
Ans. bbab.

Q.320. a___c___abb___a___bc___ab___ca
Ans. bccacb.

Q.321. ___abb___ ___bb___abb___abb___
Ans. aaaaaa.

Q.322. Roshan walks 10 metres in front and 10 metres to the right. Then everytime turning to his left he walks 5, 15 and 15 metres respectively. How far is he now from his starting point?
Ans. 5 metres.

Q.323. 'A' goes towards east 5 km, then he takes a turn south-west and goes 5 km. He again takes a turn towards north-west and goes 5 km with respect to the starting point, where is he now?
Ans. Towards west.

Q.324. If south-east becomes north, north-east becomes west and so on, what will west become?
Ans. South-east.

Q.325. A man walks 6 km to the east and then turns to the south 2 km. Again he turns to the east and walks 2 km. Next he turns northwards and walks 8 km. How far is he now from the starting point?
Ans. 10 km.

Q.326. Blend : Mix :: Abode : ?
Ans. Dwelling.

Q.327. Lend : Borrow :: Deep : ?
Ans. Shallow.

Q.328. Astrology : Future :: Nephrology : ?
Ans. Kidney.

Q.329. Power : Watt :: Weight : ?
Ans. Gram.

Q.330. Balance : Mass :: ? : Pressure
Ans. Barometer.

Q.331. Author : Book :: Dramatist : ?
Ans. Play.

Q.332. Introducing a man to her husband, a woman said, "His brother's father is the only son of my grandfather." How is man related to the woman?

Ans. Brother.

Q.333. Pointing to a man, a woman said, "His brother's father is the only son of my grandfather." How is woman related to the man?

Ans. Sister.

Q.334. A and B are brothers. C and D are sisters. A's son is D's brother. How is B related to C?

Ans. Uncle.

Q.335. If P + Q means P is the brother of Q. P × Q means P is the mother of Q. P ‚ Q means P is the sister of Q. Then R is the uncle of S can be written as how?

Ans. R + P × S.

Q.336. In a certain code CALANDER is written as CLANAEDR. How is CIRCULAR written in that code?

Ans. CRIUCALR.

Q.337. In a certain code 13479 is coded as AQFJL and 2568 is coded as DMPN. How 396824 will be coded?

Ans. QLPNDF.

Q.338. In a certain code 15789 is written as EGKPT and 2346 is written as ALUR. How is 23549 written in that code?

Ans. ALGUT.

Q.339. If PENCIL is coded as LICNEP, how INKPOT will be coded?

Ans. TOPKNI.

Q.340. Mr X started from his house, walked 2 km north, then 3 km west, then 6 km south. How far away from his house was he then?

Ans. 5 km.

Q.341. John travels 7 km eastwards, then he turns right and travels 3 km and further turns right again and travels 11 km. How far is he from the starting point?
Ans. 5 km.

Q.342. A boy walks 9 km due east and then 12 km due south. How far is he from the starting point?
Ans. 15 kms.

Q.343. P3C, R5F, T8I, V12L, (?).
Ans. X17O.

Q.344. OAL, MZN, KBP, IYR, (?).
Ans. GCT.

Q.345. A, C, F, J, (?), U.
Ans. O.

Q.346. BY, IQ, NK, QG, (?).
Ans. RE.

Q.347. CFG, EIK, GLJ, IOI, (?).
Ans. KRH.

Q.348. Q1F, S2E, U6D, W21C, (?).
Ans. Y88B.

Q.349. DKM, FJP, HIS, JHV, (?).
Ans. LGY.

Q.350. 'A is mother of B and C', and 'D is husband of C', then what is A to D?
Ans. Mother-in-law.

Q.351. A said to B that the boy swimming is the younger of the two brothers of the daughter of my father's wife. How is the boy swimming is related to A?
Ans. Brother.

Q.352. Which word describes something different from others?
ROAD   HOUSE   RESIDENCE   HOME
Ans. ROAD.

Q.353. Which word is closest in meaning to the word CONNECT?
ATTACH   DULL   FETCH   SNAP
Ans. ATTACH.

Q.354. Introducing Amit, Sakshi said, "His wife is the only sister of her father's only son." How is Amit related to Sakshi?
Ans. Husband.

Q.355. A watch reads 4:30. If the minute hand points to east, in which direction does the hour-hand point?
Ans. North-east.

Q.356. How many pairs of letters are there in the word IMPLANT which have as many letters between them as in the alphabet?
Ans. One.

Q.357. Lucknow : U.P.:: Bhopal : (?).
Ans. M.P.

Q.358. Eye : Wink : : Heart : (?).
Ans. Throb.

Q.359. QPO, SRQ, UTS, WVU, (?).
Ans. YXW.

Q.360. OTE, PUF, QVG, RWH, (?).
Ans. SXI.

Q.361. A G L P S, (?).
Ans. U.

Q.362. ABZ, BCY, CDX, DEW, (?).
Ans. EFV.

Q.363. aku, fpz, (?), pzj, ueo, zjt.
Ans. ukv.

Q.364. If the word 'STOVE' can be written as 'FNBLK', then how can the word 'VOTER' be written in that code?

Ans. LBNKF.

Explanation:
[S→F
T→N
O→B
V→L
E→K
∴ VOTES → LBNKF]

Q.365. If A = 1, FAT = 27, then FAITH = ?.

Ans. 44.

Explanation: [Faith = F + A + I + T + H = 6 + 1 + 9 + 20 + 8 = 44]

Q.366. P, Q and R are educated; P, R and S are hard working; R, S and T are employed; P, Q, S and T are polite. Who is educated, hardworking, polite but not employed?

Ans. P.

Q.367. A man starts from a point, walks 2 km towards north, turn towards his right and walks 2 km, turns right again and walks. What is the direction now he is facing?

Ans. South.

Q.368. There are some boys and dogs at a place. If total number of heads is 7 and total number of legs is 20, then how many boys and how many dogs are there?

Ans. 4 boys and 3 dogs.

Q.369. Rajiv is the brother of Atul. Sonia is the sister of Sunil. Atul is the son of Sonia. How is Rajiv related to Sonia?

Ans. Son.

Q.370. There are five friends—S, K, M, A, R; S is shorter than K, but taller than R; M is the tallest. A is a little shorter than K and little taller than S. Who has two persons taller and two persons shorter than him?

Ans. A.

Q.371. Of the five members of a panel sitting in a row, A is to the left of B, but on the right of C; D is on the right of B but is on the left of E. Find the member who is sitting in the middle?

Ans. B.

Q.372. Write the related word to complete the analogy.
genuine : authentic :: mirage : ?

Ans. Illusion.

Q.373. If '+' means '−', '−' means 'x', 'x' means ',' and means '+', then 2 , 6 × 6 , 2 = ?.

Ans. 5.

Q.374. Find the missing letters in the series:
ABC, FGH, LMN, ____.

Ans. STU.

Q.375.

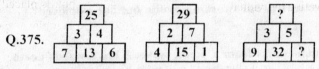

Find out the missing numbers.

Ans. 52 and 7.

Q.376. A, B, C, D and E are sitting on a bench to see the rising sun. A is to the left of C. D and E have two persons between them. E is sandwiched between B and A. Who is exactly in the middle?

Ans. A.

Q.377. In a family, the parents Anjali and Surendra have two children, Mohit and Pooja. Anjali is 2 years younger than Surendra, and Mohit two years older than Pooja. The total of their age in years is 90 and ratio between the total age of children and the total age of parents is 1:4. What is the age of Anjali?

Ans. 35 years.
Explanation: [Surendra is 37, Anjali 35, Mohit 10 and Pooja 8].

Q.378. If the digits of a two-digit number are interchanged the difference is 72. None of the digits is zero. Which is the second digit of the number?

Ans. 1.

Explanation: [91–19 = 72].

Q.379. Divide 82 apples among A, B and C so that the ratio received by A and B is 6:7 and of A and C is 4:5. How many apples will C have?

Ans. 30.

Explanation: [A = 24, B = 28 and C = 30].

Q.380. Mohan saw some beggars sitting in a row. He gave Re 1/- to the first beggar, Rs 2/- to the second beggar, Rs 3 /- to the third beggar, and so on. If the total amount given by him is Rs. 120/- how much did he give to the last beggar?

Ans. Rs 15/-.

Q.381. In how many ways can two girls and three boys sit in a line if the boys are always to be at corners and the girls will not sit together?

Ans. 12.

Q.382. How many sets of two letters in the word 'PERSONALITY' have as many letters (right or left) between them as they have in the alphabetic order?

Ans. 7. [PR, PS, RS, ON, LN, LO and OT].

Q.383. Which popular word can be formed with the 2nd, 6th, 7th, 9th and 11th letters of the word 'INTOXICATION'.

Ans. TONIC.

Q.384. Simplify: $(40^2 - 30^2) = 10 \times (?)$

Ans. 70.

Q.385. The average age of a class of 25 students is 25. If the teacher's age is also included, the average age increased by one year. What is the teacher's age?

Ans. 51 years.

Q.386. **Find the number which when added to itself 17 times, gives 162 as result.**

Ans. 9.

Q.387. **There are 27 students in a chemistry class and 22 students in a physics class. Seven of these students take physics and chemistry. What is the ratio of the number of students taking only physics to those taking chemistry?**

Ans. 3 : 4.

Q.388. **Find the missing number:**
9, 10, 13, 18, 25, (?)

Ans. 34.

Q.389. **Four bells first begin to toll together and then at intervals of 6, 7, 8 and 9 seconds respectively. Find how many times the bells toll together in two hours?**

Ans. 14 times.

Q.390. **If a shopkeeper sells an item for Rs 141, his loss is 6%. To earn a profit of 10% he should sell it for how much?**

Ans. Rs 165/-.

Q.391. **If all the letters of the word 'PERSONALITY' were arranged alphabetically, how many letters will still be where they are?**

Ans. 3.
Explanation: [E, T and Y].

Q.392. **If MARBLE is coded as NZSAMD, the code for GRANITE would be:**

Ans. HQBMJSF.
Explanation: [Letters 2, 4 and 6 .... are coded by preceding letters and the remaining by the next one].

Q.393. **A and B enter into partnership investing Rs 12,000/- and Rs 6,000/- respectively. After 8 months, C also joins the business with a capital of Rs 15,000/-. The share of C in a profit of Rs 45,600/- after 2 years will be what?**

Ans. Rs 12,000/-.

Q.394. Two numbers are respectively 25% and 40% less than the third number. What percent is the second number of the first?

Ans. 80%.

Q.395. Find the missing number:
2, 12, 30, 56, 90, ____

Ans. 132.

Q.396. A is B's brother. C is D's father. E is B's mother. A and D are brothers. How is E related to C?

Ans. Wife.

Q.397. Rama travels 10 km towards the north, turns left and travels 4 km and then again turns right and covers another 5 km and then turns right and travels another 4 km. How far is he from the starting point?

Ans. 15 km.

Q.398. Find out the number from the following that does not belong to the group for lack of common property.
(169, 289, 361, 442, 484, 729)

Ans. 442.

Explanation: [All other are square numbers].

Q.399. Find the missing number ?:

5	4	9
6	3	(?)
7	2	4
65	20	45

Ans. 01.

Explanation: $(7 + 6) \times 5 = 65$

$(2 + 3) \times 4 = 20$

$(4 + 1) \times 9 = 45$

Q.400. A sum of Rs. 6.25 P is made up of 80 coins which are either 10 P or 5 P, how many are there of each kind?

Ans. 45, 35.

Q.401. Find out the missing number.

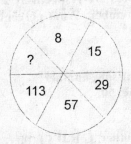

Ans. 225.

Explanation: [The numbers move CW forming a series in which the sequence is + 7, + 14, + 28, + 56, + 112).

Q.402. A word is given in capital letters. It is followed by four words. Out of the four words, three cannot be formed from the letters of the word given in capital letters. Point out that word which can be formed from the letters of the given word in capital letters—PREMONITION.

Ans. MONITOR.

Q.403. Arrange the following words according to the Dictionary.

(1) Eagle (2) Earth (3) Eager (4) Early (5) Each.

Ans. (5), (3), (1), (4), (2).

Q.404. The HCF of two numbers is 96 and their LCM is 1296. If one number is 864, then what is the other number?

Ans. 144.

Q.405. At 12:30, the hour-hand of a clock faces north and the minute-hand faces south. At 1:45, the hour-hand will be in which direction?

Ans. North-east.

Q.406. Arrange the following in a meaningful sequence:
(1) Shoulder (2) Wrist (3) Elbow (4) Palm (5) Finger.

Ans. (5), (4), (2), (3), (1).

Q.407. In a certain code, the word DEAL is coded as 4-5-1-12. Following the same rule of coding, what should be the code for the word LADY?

Ans. 12-1-4-25.

Q.408. What must be added to each term of the ratio 49: 68, so that it becomes 3:4?

Ans. 8.

Q.409. What is the smallest whole number which is divisible by 3 and also by the next two greater prime numbers?

Ans. 15.

Q.410. Anita, Mahima, Rajen, Laxmi and Dilip are five cousins. Anita is twice as old as Mahima. Rajen is half the age of Mahima. Anita is half the age of Dilip and Rajen is twice the age of Laxmi. Who is the eldest?

Ans. Dilip.

Q.411. Rearrange the following in a meaningful manner.
   I. Adolescence
   II. Infancy
   III. Puberty
   IV. Childhood
   V. Adulthood

Ans. II, IV, III, I, V.

Q.412. 19 boys turn out for hockey. Of these, 11 are wearing hockey shirts and 14 are wearing hockey pants. There are no boys without one or the other. What is the number of boys wearing full uniform?

Ans. 6.

Q.413. A watch reads 4 : 30. If the minute hand points east, then in what direction will the hour hand point?

Ans. North-east.

Q.414. When seen through a mirror, a clock shows 8 : 30. What is the correct time?

Ans. 3: 30.

Q.415. Five persons are standing in a line. One of the two persons at the extreme end is a professor and the other, a businessman. An advocate is standing to the right of a student. An author is to the left of the businessman. The student is standing between the professor and the advocate. Counting from the left, the advocate is at which place?

Ans. 3rd.

Explanation: [Professor—Student—Advocate—Author—Businessman].

Q.416. If DELHI is coded as CDKGH, then how will PATIALA be coded?

Ans. OZSHZKH.

Explanation: [Each letter moves -1 step].

Q.417. In a group of 36 persons, a total of 16 take tea while 9 take tea but not coffee. How many persons in this group take coffee but not tea?

Ans. 20.

Q.418. A group of boys decided to buy a few cassettes whose price was between Rs. 200 and Rs. 250. But at the time of purchase, two of the boys declined to contribute as a result of which the remaining boys had to pay Rupee 1 more than they had originally planned. What was the price of the cassettes if the boys contributed equally and in whole number of rupees?

Ans. Rs 220/-.

Chapter three

Language Skills and Comprehension

Boss Series

Paragraph Writing

I. ROLE OF GAMES IN SCHOOL CURRICULUM

Sport is a physical activity carried out especially outdoors for exercise, amusements or as a past time, usually played in a special area and in accordance with rules. It has remained an integral part of human life since the beginning of the evolutionary process. Nobody knows exactly how or when sport started and developed in society. But it has been spread throughout the world among all species by nature itself. The quality of participation is inherent in human psyche.

Over the ages through human evolution the urge and need to know about life itself and the environment surrounding it have also evolved. Man has developed a systematic study of nature. But somehow the essence of life as sport has lost its importance and meaning. Education has been established as reading, writing and applying certain facts and procedures for selling and buying products manufactured by wealthy people. Sport has taken a secondary role for extra-curricular activity of students.

In new millennium sports has to be given a new status in our whole education system. No nation can develop to its possible potential unless the citizens of the nation are healthy and fit enough to carry out the designated work. The sole aim of sports in our education system is the harmonious development of the child and the word 'harmonious' development means a child is fit in all respects, i.e., physically, mentally, socially and emotionally.

If we pay attention, the academic subjects, viz, physics, chemistry, biology and psychology are all ingredients of sports apart from all other conceivable subjects like history, geography, economics, international understanding. Instead of trying to teach various subjects, if all children were allowed to play and learn sports through various influencing factors, society would have looked absolutely different.

Sports is the most integral part of the general education through physical activities. It includes large muscles activities to develop and control the different parts of the body through movements. Performing different types of movement teaches us to co-ordinate mind and body. Thus, sports help in developing the sense of working in the group which in turn teaches a child to behave in the society.

Sports are associated with the joy of success and fear of failure which teaches an individual to control the emotional stage and also teaches a child how to react in a given situation. Thus, inculcating sports in school curriculum will help in developing physical health, mental soundness, self-confidence and ultimately the social growth. We should never forget the proverb which say:

"All work, and no play makes Jack a dull boy." It would be boring for school children to study all the time. Games and sports provide them with recreation and relaxation. Hence we conclude by saying:

'Only healthy people benefit
Mankind the mother Earth—
Others are a burden.'

II. NEED TO DEVELOP SPORTS CULTURE IN INDIA

A constantly increasing interest in sports has become a global phenomenon. Growing health care awareness among people, and also print and electronic media projections of sports have further contributed to their popularity. The demand for making physical education and sports as an integral part of the curriculum is gaining momentum.

The "UNESCO International Charter on Physical Education and Sports" adopted in 1978 has called upon all countries to make the right to physical education and sports as a fundamental right. Undoubtedly implementation of this cardinal principles in developing countries like India is not feasible because of a lack of financial resources. Hence attention has to be paid to it.

Let us start with the dual understanding, one that sports have enough potential to motivate masses to participate in one or the other category of sports, and two, that there is total unanimity among all the citizen including the concerned authorities, that the sports need adequate promotion in our country.

Today, almost all champion Indian sports persons are the production of their self-effort and body potentials without getting any orderly guidance from the sports/physical education institutional coaches/ teachers. Therefore, to broadbase sports and physical activities, it is high time to improve the quality of production of our coaches and physical educators.

In addition, we must understand that in today's scientific world there is strong need to broadbase and strengthen the research and development in physical education and sports, so as to remain ever updated and properly equipped with day-to-day developments in this field. As a result, the application of modern science and technology to analyse and improve performance in sport is constantly thrust in. Until a few decades ago sport in India was viewed as the direct control of religious teachers. As the modern technology, urbanisation and economic globalisation paced up in way of life, sport has dramatically replaced as intergrated part of rapidly changing society. Now sport is considered as a profession, a work place. Enlighted companies have started sponsoring sports, teams, and in some instances, have provided fields at their worksites. Such initiatives were viewed mainly as a method of building a team spirit and increasing employee morale. These initiatives can enhance the performance of the employee.

During the last two decades physical education in India has taken grand strides. With the opening of a number of physical education colleges and university departments with more emphasis on post-graduate studies, a new phase has begun which is indicative of a sort of "awakening" within the profession. It now seems certain that our educationists, planners and policy makers as well as political masters are convinced of the efficiency of this discipline.

In India physical education is becoming a well-established profession but still many steps have to be taken to improve the standard of sports in our country.

First and foremost, there is a need to set up separate policies related to sports. Sports should be considered an important agenda for the Planning Commissions. Authorities should gear up the district-level tribal and rural areas sports bodies, so that they work more efficiently and help in searching and developing new sports talents.

Thus, with the rising 'sports' culture in India we can certainly think of India with bright and prosperous future.

III. SPORTS SCIENCES—AN EMERGING DISCIPLINE

Human society is dynamic and so are its needs. Our volatile lifestyles and sedentary nature of job profiles leave us in a state of physical, mental and social fatigue. We feel leeched and worn out owing to mundane corporate schedules. In the modern computer age, where we rely more on our mental faculties and machines for our work, we certainly can't ignore our body that is the instrument of our mind. There has to be a correct balance between mental pursuits and physical activity.

Sports sciences is a blanket term and encompasses virtually each aspect and domain of one's life. Sports is an activity that is institutionalized in nature and demands demonstration of the physical prowess, associating it with 'sciences' further making it more meaningful, i.e., now it can be considered as the study of all facilities ranging from physical, mental, spiritual and other elusive sublimations of human body. Giving it a wider perspective, discipline of sports sciences aim at developing and attainment of high level of proficiency of speed, strength, endurance and co-ordinative abilities.

Sports sciences as a discipline fulfils the long desired goal of striking the right balance amongst various endeavours in an individual. Now-a-days, emphasis is being laid on overall development of the child and that objective can be achieved only if sports sciences are incorporated as an integral discipline at school and undergraduate levels at least. Being a receptive phase of life, the learner tends to imbible those techniques, methods and virtues that would mould his lifestyle thereafter throughout his life.

Be it administrator, coach, sports scientist, they are giving a wider dimension to sports in our daily lives and in ultra modern infrastructures, a specialized approach would prove to be instrumental in attainment of wider objectives. So, nitty gritty of the matter is that sports sciences is emerging as a rising, shining and prevalent discipline that will certainly instil constructive nature to the intelligent human creature. So, we can say sport science build that foundation standing tall on which one can face and meet that challenges and fatigue inducing demands more efficiently.

IV. RURAL SPORTS IN PUNJAB

In villages which formed the first habitation of civilised man rural sports grew out of sheer necessity. The need for cultivating individual strength for labour on the fields, the interdependence within the community and need of defence, joint defence against onslaughts of a common foe and dangerous animals must have given birth to sports like wrestling, running, jumping, weightlifting and such performing arts as of measuring strength by holding wrists, twisting hands. Kabaddi which is another expression of the same spirit has become the mother of games in Punjab.

In order to toughen the frames and steel the minds of his followers Guru Hargobindji had started the tradition of holding wrestling bouts within the precincts of Akal Takht Sahib and it is mostly because of the filip that he gave and the seal of ethics that he put on them that sports become a proud facet of life in Punjab. On the common grounds of villages, in the fairs, during the festivals, at the hermitages of pirs, graves of preceptors, wrestling became a part of high recreation. Villages adopt and feed wrestlers and also give prizes to them as a matter of honour in Punjab today.

During the Hola Mohalla celebrations at Anandpur Sahib tent pegging competitions, archery, fencing and riding competitions, gymnastic and acrobatic displays which the Nihangs put up and the tournaments held at Diwali have a hoary history. To the Punjabis goes the distinction of organizing rural games in tournaments.

Almost sixty years ago when the Grewal Sports Association had begun to hold competitions in rural sports at Village Quilla Raipur little would have anyone thought that this tournament will become a movement in Punjab.

Today in almost 7000 villages in Punjab in one decade or the other rural sports competitions are being held. Rural folk organize them. It is they who extend all hospitality to the competitors also. In fact these village sports have opened the floodgates of village development.

Before independence in 1947 major importance was given only to kabaddi and wrestling, after independence the circle of rural sports also got widened. The rustic "Khido Khoondi" (literally a ball made out of cuttings of cloth and a stick twisted at the end like a flat hockey blade) was replaced by proper hockey and players from villages, having no facilities beyond uneven grounds to play began to dominate in the game. Twelve of our country's greatest hockey players have come out of a single village called Sansarpur in Jalandhar District.

Recently not only revival of sports fairs has taken place in Punjab but their number has also increased tremendously. Twenty years ago, for instance, their number was limited to:

* Babehali-di-Chhinj
* Bhaggowal-di-Chhinj
* Shikar-Macchian di-Parewi
* Jaura-Chhatra-di-Parewi
* Bhomey-Wadaley-di-Chhinj
* Quilla Raipur's sports
* Shanker-di-Chhinj
* Munum-honey-di-Chhinj, etc.

Now sports meets are held almost in every significant village in Punjab.

Three types of competitions are held during rural meets, purely rural games: Kabaddi, Wrestling, Weight-lifting, etc; modern sports like athletics, hockey, football, volleyball, cycling, handball, etc. and performing sports like acrobatics, twisting an iron-rod by placing it on Adam's apple, passing tractor over the rib-ease, cracking a big stone by placing it on the chest, etc. Now another colour is also being added to these sports fairs. They have got intermixed with folk singing when sun sets after the days sports competitions the notes of music begin to emanate and singing continues, sometimes, late in the night.

Music contest that was held between Karamjit Dhuri and Jagmohan Kaur at Kila Raipur is still fondly remembered. At the Gujarwal Meet the singing of Parminder Sandhu, Hans Raj Hans and Surinder Chhinda and at fairs of Majha region the notes O Toombi (one-stringed instrument) of Amarjit remain fixed in the minds of the people.

Villagers are not just fond of their own competitions they also like to size-up the skill and power of their animals like bulls, horses, dogs on the sports ground. Bullockcart racing has become a passion in Punjab. Because of a ban on hunting, hound-races are held in Punjab by dangling a bait of fake hare before them. At places cock-fights are also held and pigeon fights are contested. In some parts of Punjab people indulge in fighting a bull by barehands.

Rural sports are a personification of the virility of Punjab.

V. HOCKEY: HOW TO PLAY?

Hockey is a popular sports for men and women in many countries around the world. It is simply known as hockey in most countries, especially those in which ice hockey is not very prominent.

Hockey has several regular, prestigious international tournaments for both men and women such as the Olympic Games, the quadrennial World Hockey Cups, the annual Champions Trophies, and World Cups for juniors.

Indian and Pakistani National teams have traditionally dominated men's hockey, but have become less prominent recently, with Australia, The Netherlands, and Germany the strongest since the 1980s. The Netherlands was the predominant international women's team before hockey was added to Olympic events. In the early 1990s Australia emerged as the strongest women's country, though retirement of a number of key players has weakened the team.

Hockey is the oldest known stick-and-ball game (perhaps apart from Irish Hurling which dates back to pre-historic times). Historical records show that games resembling modern field hockey were played in various ancient civilizations, although it is not possible to know exactly when and where the game began. While *Modern hockey* appears in the mid-18th century in England, primarily around schools, it is not until the first half of the 19th century that hockey became firmly established, when the first club, Blackheath, is created in 1849 in south-east London, England.

In the early 1970s, artificial turf fields began to be used in competition. The introduction of the synthetic pitches instead of the grass ones has completely changed most aspects of hockey. The game, as well as the material used to play, have taken a definitive turn, gaining mainly in speed. In order to take into account the specificities of this surface, new tactics, new techniques have been developed and new rules have been settled, often, in order to frame this new technique.

The game is played between two teams of eleven players on a 100 × 60 yard (91 × 55 metre) rectangular field. At each end there is a goal approximately 7 feet (2.1 metres) high and 12 feet (3.6 metres) wide, and a semi-circle 16 yards (15 metres) from the goal known as the "arc", or "shooting circle", with a dotted line 5 yards from the semi-circle, as well as lines across the field 25 yards (23 metres) from each end-line and in the centre of the field. A spot, called the penalty spot, is placed 7 yards from the center of each goal.

Each player carries a "stick", normally a little over 3 feet long and traditionally made of wood but now often made with fibreglass, kevlar and carbon fibre composites, with a rounded handle flattening out on one side and with a hook at the bottom. The flat side of the hook is used to push, dribble, or hit a hard plastic ball. Each field player normally wears a mouth and shin guards. A goalkeeper must wear complete protective gear: normally a helmet, neck guard, chest protector, gloves, super-padded shin guards, and kickers which cover their feet and allow them to kick the ball.

Players are only permitted to play the ball with the flat side or edges of the stick. The fat side is always on the "natural" side for a right-handed person—there are no "left-handed" hockey sticks. If the ball is raised off the ground in a manner that is in the umpires opinion dangerous the ball is turned over to the other team and they receive a free hit from the point of contact. Balls travelling at head height near players are almost always regarded as dangerous, whereas a flick at knee height landing into space would very rarely be so. When shooting at goal any height is permitted as it is a shoot on goal; as long as it is not dangerous to a player within 3 yards (about 3 metres) of the striker.

One player from each team is designated the "goalkeeper", and is permitted to play the ball with any part of their body whilst within their defensive circle (the arc). Goalkeepers do have a stick which is primarily used for dives.

If a defence field player commits one of the many fouls (kicking the ball, obstruction, lifting in a dangerous area, back side of the stick, etc.) inside their defensive shooting circle, or commits a deliberate or particularly serious foul outside the circle but within their defensive quarter of the field, then a complicated and indirect penalty shot is taken, called a "penalty corner". A deliberate breach by defenders within the circle, or a rule breach that directly prevents a goal being scored, results in the award of a "penalty stroke", approximately equivalent to a penalty shot in soccer.

The match is officiated by two umpires. Each umpire generally controls half of the field. The teams' object is to play the ball into their "shooting circle" and, from there, hit or push the ball into the goal. The team with more goals after two 35-minute halves wins the game.

VI. INTERNATIONAL OLYMPIC COMMITTEE (IOC)

The International Olympic Committee (IOC) is an organization based in Lausanne, Switzerland, created by Pierre de Coubertin in 1894 to reinstate the Ancient Olympic Games held in Greece, and organize this sports event every four years. The IOC receives its operating funds through advertising and merchandising Olympic memorabilia, as well as through sale of rights to the media who report on the occurrences at the Olympic Games.

On June 23, 1894 the Olympic Games were re-created by Pierre de Coubertin after a hiatus of 1500 years. The baron hoped to foster international communication and peace through the Olympic Games. The IOC is a parent organization intended to localize administration and authority for the Games, as well as to provide a single legal entity which owns copyrights, trademarks, and other intangible properties associated with the Olympic Games. For example, the Olympic logos, the design of the Olympic flag, the motto, creed, and anthem are all owned and administered by the IOC. There are other organizations which the IOC coordinates as well, which are collectively called the Olympic Movement. The IOC President is responsible for representing the IOC as a whole, and there are members of the IOC which represent the IOC in their respective countries.

Countries which wish to host the Summer Olympic Games or the Winter Olympic Games must bid for the organization with the IOC, which has the ultimate authority of deciding where the Games will take place. The IOC members, representing most of the member countries, vote to decide where the Games will take place. By law, all IOC members must retire at the age of 81. Members from countries which have cities bidding to host the Games are excluded from the voting processes, up until the point where their city drops out of the contest.

The IOC has been involved in a number of scandals, most involving members taking advantage of the bidding cities to extort financial and other rewards. The most widely publicised example occurred in relation to the 2002 Winter Olympics in Salt Lake City. After the Salt Lake City scandal, efforts were made to clamp down on the most blatant misbehaviour of IOC delegates (who used their position as voters for the host city to extract favours from bidders for the Games), and an advisory board of recently retired former athletes has been set up. Critics of the organization believe more fundamental reform is required, for instance, replacing the self-perpetuating system of delegate selection with a more democratic process.

VII. SPORTS CAREERS IN AMERICA

Sports, the very word gives a feeling of games, fun, some physical activities and probably, that's all. Yes, that is all for a layman. But if an effort is put in to really know the real picture which this vast, and dynamic field has, it's only then that we can realise the academic importance and career options it has to offer.

To begin with, Athletic Training play a key role in the rehabilitation of a world-class athlete. Barry's Bachelor of Science degree program in Athletic Training is one of the first two programs in the United States to receive national accreditation by CAAHEP

Today, emerging careers in fitness, wellness and cardiopulmonary rehabilitation have increased the need for professionals with expertise in the field.

Exercise Science—The BS degree program helps the sports lover to be a fitness instructor and seek positions in corporations, hospitals and fitness centers as they pursue certification from the American College of Sports Medicine (ACSM).

To add more, a major in physical education prepares a person to participate in the Florida Teacher Certification Examination (FTCE) which further has 2 options, one of the K-8 state certification or another leading to state teaching certification for grades 6-12. These qualifications are fit to help a first grader develop motor coordination, improve the fitness level of a middle-schooler, or coach a high school in basketball team to victory! Going on further, we can talk of the career in sports management. It's for those who have dreamt of being an Athletic Director, operating a major resort, owning a sport-related business, and managing a health and fitness facility, and to live up to these dreams, they simply have to do a Bachelor of Science in Sport Management. This degree prepares the candidate for event management, public relations, professional sport, and marketing.

And if all this seems less, then just to mention a few more are the careers in Aerobic specialist, Aquatic and swimming specialist, Armed forces physical education specialist, Athletic coach, High school physical education teacher, Junior high school physical education teacher, Senior fitness specialist, Sports camp supervisors, and the list continues. So, once the numerous opportunities are explored in the field of sports, the notion that it's just a physical activity or probably some knowledge of games is completely washed away.

VIII. HEALTH AND WELLNESS

Childhood obesity levels are rising and children today are significantly heavier than they were in previous decades. This is mainly due to children being less active than their predecessors and eating the wrong kinds of foods. This state of affairs could lead to serious health problems in the long term. Yet, the key habits of maintaining good health—eating healthily and staying physically active—should be established in childhood and parents can play a vital role in securing the future health of their children.

Two of the key factors contributing to obesity are poor diet and lack of physical activity. The National Diet and Nutrition Survey of young people aged 4-18 years found that children were eating less than half the recommended five portions of fruit and vegetables each day and one in five ate no fruit at all. Over 80 percent of those surveyed regularly ate foods such as white bread, savoury snacks, chocolate confectionery, chips and biscuits. As far as physical activity is concerned, they found that 40-69 percent of children over the age of six years are largely inactive, spending less than one hour per day participating in moderate-intensity activities.

A report produced by the British Medical Association (BMA) in December 2003 on Adolescent Health painted a similar picture and highlighted the importance of establishing healthy habits early in childhood. The report showed a disturbing trend in teens to be obese and have a host of unhealthy lifestyle habits, such as smoking and drinking. According to the report, one in five young people aged between 13 and 16 years is overweight and less than 15 percent of girls aged 13 to 15 years eat the recommended amounts of fruit and vegetables. In fact, the report authors say, "Obesity has come to be considered as a global epidemic and excess body weight is now the most common childhood disorder in Europe."

Parents can make a huge impact on rising levels of childhood obesity. The good news is that the evidence shows parents can successfully treat their child's obesity by actively changing the whole family's approach to diet and physical activity by avoiding couch potato lifestyles.

Good nutritional practices and physical activity should be encouraged as early as possible in children's lives before unhealthy habits become established. It appears, for example that access and exposure to a range of fruit and vegetables in the home is important for the development of preferences for those foods. Additionally, parental knowledge, attitudes and behaviours related to healthy diet and physical activity are important in creating role models.

Helping children to develop healthier lifestyles in their early years is an important step to prevent excess weight gain. There are many ways to combat the growing problem of obesity. These include providing children with a healthy, varied, balanced diet rich in fruit and vegetables both at schools and at home, as well as increasing physical activity levels both at school and outside school, which will improve their overall health and well-being.

Children should be active for 30-60 minutes per day at a moderate intensity, such as brisk walking. They should participate in activities that will enhance and maintain strength, flexibility and bone strength; skipping, and dancing at least twice a week will surely help in achieving this objective.

IX. SPORTS AS A PROFESSION

Whenever professions are being talked about, the belief that acquiring a medical, engineering, or a management degree is akin to having made one's career. These are the widely known, accepted and pursued careers since long now. Also the parents look upto only these professions as their child's career. But did we ever stop and wonder— why? Why only these or may be a few more after this are said to be the right choices for a good career. Why not a career in sports? Why not a sport professional is preferred?

Well, the main cause behind it is the mindset of all, which have been made by the communication channels through which the informations on all these travel effectively and also the opportunities for pursuing academics and later on, a job to settle in are provided extensively. And in the same regard, when we talk of sports, then the institutes offering courses, the details of all the courses, the placement cells (if any), the career growth and status—all this and more is required by anyone who wants to have or is to be motivated for a carrer in sports. But the hard and disappointing fact is, the informations do not travel effectively and the opportunities are not conveyed widely, which certainly results in hesitation from all fronts as everybody seeks for security in profession they would want to pursue. When we come to talk of it, then it talks of Athletic directors, Athletic coaches, Aerobic specialists, Aquatic and swimming specialists, Junior High School Physical Education Teachers, Senior High School Physical Education Teachers, not only this but we have sports journalists, sports photographers, and the list goes on. All these and much more opportunities are available and all require specially trained staff with required courses to be taken and have a world of opportunities waiting for them.

Apart from this, various other mental blocks and the notions should be broken. Certain concepts have made a permanent mark in everyone's mind like, it's only medical, or engineering, a big amount of respect attached, it's only these which have stability for life and good money flowing in, but it's not absolutely a true fact. In reference to sports, as well, we can say that all the above is true.

Lastly, one thing that's really important and majorly ignored is the fact, that a profession or a career line should not be only about earning a bread, it's all about one's interest, one's skills and one's need of all kinds from a career that is to be considered for a happy professional life. So, all in all, sports as a profession is certainly a respectable, facilitating earning for life profession. One with the right aptitude for it, should certainly pursue it and the communication on the same needs some more attention, so that the mental blocks in the minds can be removed.

X. CRICKET CRAZE IN INDIA

Cricket is a craze! Cricket is a religion! Cricketers are demi-gods! Indeed cricket has become a way of life in the country of more than 100 billion populations. No other game had ever been so powerful as cricket in India. And India has become a cricketing super power!

The Board of Control for Cricket in India (BCCI) is a much richer body than the International Cricket Council! And this passion and associated affluence has made India a great power in the world cricket. No wonder, there is a mad rush to cash in on the wide popularity of the game! Cricketers are considered as the best brand ambassadors. Irfan Pathan, hardly two years old in the international cricket, has grown into a big catch for the industry to promote products. Sachin Tendulkar is revered. Saurav Ganguly is worshipped. Sehwag is chased and the description could be unending. Cricket tournaments are like big occasions that nobody would want to miss. And perhaps in the mad race for sponsorship, 1996 Wills World Cricket Cup became a battle ground for the two US cola giants. As Coca Cola walked away with the prestigious sponsorship to project Coke as the official drink. Pepsi came out as a winner with its stars among Indian cricket team to sweep the competitors off their feet by an attractive campaign— "Pepsi—Nothing official about it."

Some believe that England is the only country where cricket is played. However, that is not true; it happens to be the most popular sport in India. There are many other main countries besides England and India which participate in this sport. They include Australia, South Africa, Zimbabwe, Pakistan, Sri Lanka, New Zealand and the West Indies. There are a total of 32 countries that are a member of the International Cricket Council.

Cricket is the national game of England and several other countries. Cricket has been there ever since most Englishmen can remember. So, how did it get to these other countries? England colonized most countries that participate in international cricket. When the English colonized these different countries, they brought their traditions and sports with them. Once England was "kicked out" of these countries, many of their traditions stayed. A lot of these countries' culture today reflects back to the time of English rule. One of these traditions is Cricket. This is one way, that cricket spread, although there are many different reasons for cricket being where it is today.

Today if you open an Indian magazine and flip to the sports sections, you will see a lot of cricket news. Unfortunately, this news is bad news. Recently, there have been five Indian players banned from playing in cricket matches. This is because of match fixing. Match fixing is when, teams in advance bribe each other to win or lose certain games. The five players, former captain, Muhammad Azharuddin, Nayan Mongia, Ajay Jadeja, Manoj Prabhakar and Ajay Sharma, deny their participation in such a thing and contend that the police were misinformed. The police are now reviewing the incident and are considering a different punishment for them instead of banning them for life from cricket.

Cricket has changed the world in many ways. It has helped unite the world. It has brought countries together for different competitions. Team sports, like cricket, not only bring countries together, they also bring people together and help them learn to work together.

XI. ROLE OF GAMES AND SPORTS

Someone said, "The way a person plays a game tells me about his character, and the way he loses tell me everything". It's rightly said and says a lot about the role, sports has to play in an individual's growth and won't be wrong to say that in turn plays a great deal in nation's growth. The question that arises here, 'What has a nation done for the development of sports?', after realizing its importance in contributing to a healthy and fit nation.

Let's talk of the tradition of sports and physical fitness, and its following development, in reference to our nation—INDIA. To begin with, INDIA, in recognition of the importance of sports, a separate department was set up in 1982, subsequently, the first ever National Sports Policy was announced in 1984. Later SAI—Sports Authority of India—was established in 1984 with objective of optimum utilisation of various sports facilities and all matters related to its promotion and management. Not only this, but SAI also contributes towards the development of sports through various programmes.

First—the Main Schemes—To mention a few programmes and activities of SAI, it has National Sports Talent Contest (NSTC), Sports Project Development Area (SPDA), National Coaching Scheme, and many such more schemes under it.

Secondly—There has been a major role of *academics in the field of sports.* Majorly responsible are the two functional wings:-

i. Netaji Subhash National Institution of Sports (NSNIS), which conducts academic courses for training of coaches, and

ii. LNIPE that offers a 3-year B.P.E. and a 2-year M.P.E. degree courses which are bachelors and masters respectively in physical education.

Thirdly in the same regard are the remarkable initiatives being taken by the business undertakings, state governments, local statutory bodies, UT administration etc. by offering schemes of grants for its infrastructure, grants to rural schools, for playfields and sports equipment. The infrastructure has been given a big boost in all spheres.

Lastly are the introduction and honours in form of the various rewards and prestigious awards that are given to all the deserving sportspersons, who have done, are doing and will keep doing our nation (and all others) proud!

To conclude, the belief that sports helps in or plays a role in shaping of the physical, mental and spiritual character of an individual, of a nation, and in turn, is also given the right shape at right time by the individual, by the nation, would be the appropriate note to end on.

XII. शारीरिक शिक्षा एवम् खेल पाठ्यक्रम का अभिन्न अंग होना चाहिए

आज से लगभग 50 वर्ष पूर्व तक कहा जाता थाः

> "खेलोगे-कूदोगे होगे खराब।
> पढ़ोगे-लिखोगे बनोगे नवाब।।"

लेकिन अब समय बदल गया है। लोगों की संकीर्ण मानसिकता में बदलाव आया है। आज का हर बच्चा सचिन तेंदुलकर, सहवाग, लैंडर पेस, रोनाल्डो, सान्या मिर्जा बनना चाहता है। अतः लोगों के दृष्टिकोण में जो परिवर्तन आया है, उसकी वज़ह से पाठ्यक्रम में शारीरिक शिक्षा को महत्व दिया जाए, इसके लिए प्रयास करना ज़रूरी है। आज खिलाड़ी होने में लोग गर्व का अनुभव करते हैं। खिलाड़ी होना श्रेष्ठता का पर्याय हो गया है। खिलाड़ी को विद्यालयों, कालेजों में प्रवेश आसानी से मिल जाता है। नौकरियों की सुविधाएँ भी उपलब्ध हैं। खेल को जब लोग कैरियर के रूप में चुनने लगे हैं तो अच्छा होगा यदि आरम्भ से ही पाठ्यक्रम में इसको अनिवार्य विषय के रूप में शामिल किया जाए।

वैसे भी शिक्षा का उद्देश्य-जीवन का सभी प्रकार से विकास करना है। यह विकास जितना मन मस्तिष्क का आवश्यक है उतना ही शरीर का भी आवश्यक है। केवल किताबी कीड़ा बनने से कुछ परीक्षाएँ तो पास की जा सकती हैं पर तन-मन और बुद्धि का सम्पूर्ण विकास शारीरिक शिक्षा के बिना संभव नहीं।

खेल कूद हमें जीवन में बहुत कुछ सिखाते हैं। ये हमारे जीवन के क्रम और व्यवहार को ठीक करते हैं। हर प्रकार का परिश्रम कर भविष्य में पूर्ण बनाने का सफल प्रयास करना सिखाते हैं। मिल जुल कर काम कर लक्ष्य तक पहुँचने की प्रेरणा देते हैं, विजय पाने की लालसा को प्रबल बनाते हैं। कहने का तात्पर्य है कि खेल शरीर, मन और आत्मा के विकास के सुंदर साधन हैं।

आज जो धर्म के नाम पर आए दिन सांप्रदायिक दंगे-फसाद होते हैं वर्ग-भेद और जाति-भेद की देश के सामने जो ज्वलंत समस्या है। कभी अयोध्या में तो कभी पंजाब में, कभी गुजरात में तो कभी जम्मू-कश्मीर में आए दिन जो मानवता का क्रूर रूप हमारे सामने आता है उन सबसे मुक्त होने का साधन है खेल-कूद। इसमें व्यक्तिगत भेद-भाव को भूलकर उस खिलाड़ी को गले का हार बना लेते हैं जो हमारा दिल जीत लेता है। पढ़ाई लिखाई आदमी की आँखें खोलकर उसे अंधेरे से उजाले की

तरफ ले जाती है तो खेल-कूद तन को दुर्बलता और रोगों से बचाकर सबलता और निरोगता की ओर ले जाता है।

आजकल समाचार पत्रों में जब पढ़ते हैं तो देखते हैं कि दिल का दौरा पढ़ने से, रक्तचाप के बढ़ने से, किडनी और लीवर के नष्ट होने से कितने व्यक्ति पहले की अपेक्षाकृत अधिक मृत्यु की चपेट में आ रहे हैं। इन सबका कारण है अपने शरीर के संबंध में उचित जानकारी का अभाव। यदि आरम्भ से ही शारीरिक शिक्षा को पाठ्यक्रम का अभिन्न अंग बनाया जाए तो शायद यह नौबत न आएगी।

खेल-कूद मन रमाने का ढंग है। खिलाड़ी खेल के मैदान में खेलते हुए शेष दुनिया के तनावों को भूल जाते हैं। उनका ध्यान गेंद, फुटबॉल या खेल में लीन रहता है। कैरम, ताश, शतरंज आदि खेलों से बौद्धिक विकास के साथ-साथ मनोरंजन भी होता है।

प्राचीन काल में भी ऋषि-मुनियों के आश्रम में शारीरिक शिक्षा पर बल दिया जाता था। राजकुमारों को भी शारीरिक बल बढ़ाने के लिए पाठ्यक्रम में यह विषय अनिवार्य रूप से शामिल किया जाता था। अर्जुन को महाभारत के युद्ध में जाने से पूर्व वेद व्यास ने शक्ति संचार करने का परामर्श दिया था, तो क्या हम अपनी संस्कृति से नाता तोड़ लें—जी नहीं।

अतः खेल-कूद, शारीरिक शिक्षा पाठ्यक्रम का अनिवार्य अंग होना चाहिए।

XIII. योग शिक्षा

भारत में प्राचीन काल से योग प्रचलित है। योग विद्या सम्पूर्ण जीवन-दर्शन है। योग केवल शारीरिक स्वास्थ्य मात्र न होकर परम् तत्व की अनुभूति है। इसके द्वारा सर्वांगीण विकास, संयमित, शान्त एवं संतुलित समाज का निर्माण किया जा सकता है। योग—एक जीवन है और इसको अपनाना जीवन-कला है।

योग शब्द की उत्पत्ति संस्कृत भाषा के "युजिर" से हुई है, जिसका अर्थ है बाँधना, युक्त होना, सम्मिलित होना, एक होना। योग द्वारा हम शरीर, मन और आत्मा की सम्रग शक्तियों को संयोजित कर, जीवन का निर्वाह कर सकते हैं। कहा जाता है कि योग द्वारा चेतना निश्चेष्ट हो जाती है, मन शान्त हो जाता है, बुद्धि अचंचल हो जाती है, तब ज्ञान द्वारा सर्वोच्च पद प्राप्त होता है। जिसे हम योग-जीवन की संज्ञा देते हैं।

योग विज्ञान से प्रभावित होकर पाश्चात्य जगत ने भी योग को अपनाया है। निरे भौतिकतावाद से उब चुका पश्चिमी समाज अब योग-साधना से जुड़ रहा है और उसके सार्थक परिणाम प्राप्त हुए हैं।

अंततः योग विज्ञान है, जीवन शैली है और जीने की कला है।

XIV. इण्टरनैट : एक आवश्यकता

आज के इस आपाधापी के युग में किसी भी व्यक्ति को इतनी फुर्सत नहीं कि वह बैठकर एक पत्र लिखने का भी समय निकाल सके। इस कम्प्यूटर युग में इण्टरनैट सर्वसुलभ साधन है। इस साधन से व्यस्ततम् जीवन जीने वाला आज का मानव अपने किसी सात समुद्र पार विदेशस्थ बन्धु-बान्धव को अपनी बात पलों में कह सकता है। यद्यपि दूरभाष से भी सम्पर्क साधा जा सकता है, तथापि इण्टरनैट के द्वारा ई मेल भेजकर तत्काल बातचीत हो सकती है तथा अपने उस आत्मीय को प्रत्यक्ष देखा भी जा सकता है।

इण्टरनैट ने आज विश्वभर में बहुत बड़ा परिवर्तन ला दिया है। वस्तुतः इससे सर्वत्र क्रान्ति आ गई है। इण्टरनैट का आगमन यद्यपि चुपके से हुआ है तथापि अब तो इससे सम्पूर्ण विश्व आबद्ध हो चुका है।

एक युवा दम्पती ने अपने घर से अपने किसी एक मित्र के घर दूर विदेश में अपना सम्पर्क स्थापित करना चाहा। उस युवा दम्पती को उस स्थान का तनिक भी भौगोलिक ज्ञान नहीं था, परन्तु उन्हें कुछ क्षणों में ही मानचित्रों सहित उस दूरी की सूचना लघुतम मार्ग द्वारा प्राप्त हो गई। यह कार्य इण्टरनैट की बदौलत अत्यन्त शीघ्र हो गया।

कम्प्यूटर का एक प्रोग्राम अटलाण्टा में शाम को छः बजे प्रारम्भ होता है। यह प्रोग्राम इण्टरनैट के द्वारा अपना सारा रिकार्ड लन्दन स्थित शाखा कार्यालय में कुछ पलों में ही पहुँचा देता है।

यही नहीं, अपितु आप भारत में हैं और आपके पोते का जन्म अमेरिका में हुआ है तो आपको उसके जन्म लेते ही इण्टरनैट के द्वारा सूचना प्राप्त हो जाएगी।

आज विदेशों में और भारत में सर्वत्र इण्टरनैट का प्रयोग हो रहा है। क्या घर, क्या कार्यालय, क्या महाविद्यालय, क्या विद्यालय, क्या बैंक, क्या प्राइवेट कम्पनियाँ तथा क्या विश्वविद्यालय—प्रायः सब जगह इण्टरनैट की सुविधा उपलब्ध है।

आपको यह जानकर अत्यन्त आश्चर्य होगा कि वैज्ञानिक तो सन् 1980 से इण्टरनैट का प्रयोग कर रहे हैं।

इण्टरनैट के द्वारा बहुत कुछ सीखा जा सकता है। यदि आप अपना बिल, आवेदन पत्र अथवा कोई भी महत्वपूर्ण मसौदा किसी सरकारी कार्यालय में देना चाहते हैं तो आप को पंक्ति में खड़े होकर अब घण्टों प्रतीक्षा नहीं करनी पड़ेगी। यह काम तत्काल इण्टरनैट के द्वारा हो जाता है। इस प्रकार किसी भी सूचना को प्राप्त करने के लिये इण्टरनैट की सहायता से तत्क्षण कार्य-सिद्धि हो जाती है।

इण्टरनैट आज की एक सबसे बड़ी आवश्यकता है। आज सम्प्रेषण का सबसे सरल और शीघ्रतम माध्यम इण्टरनैट है। अत्यन्त महत्वपूर्ण बात यह है कि इण्टरनैट कई रहस्यों का उद्घाटन करता है और तकनीकी कार्य कैसे होते हैं, इसे समझाने के लिये सहायता करता है।

संक्षेप में इण्टरनैट के लाभ हैं–(1) यह संचार का साधन है। (2) मनोरंजन का साधन है। (3) उद्योग, वाणिज्य, व्यापार, व्यवसाय आदि के लिये अत्यन्त उपयोगी है। (4) किसी भी प्रकार की सूचना के लिये सर्वाधिक सहायता प्रदान करने वाला है। (5) इसके द्वारा सारा विश्व मानो सिमटकर एक जगह पर आ जाता है। इससे सारा विश्व मानो एक मुट्ठी में कैद हो जाता है।

चिकित्सा-सम्बन्धी सारे कार्य इण्टरनैट के द्वारा शीघ्रातिशीघ्र हो जाते हैं। वस्तुतः यह सूचना का भण्डार है। यह असीम है। राष्ट्रों की सीमा से परे है। इसका चरित्र अन्तर्राष्ट्रीय है। यह दृश्य, श्रव्य और पाठ्य-तीनों प्रकार की सूचनाओं का साधन है।

XV. वर्तमान भारत की ज्वलन्त समस्याएँ

एक राष्ट्र, जो अपने आप में विविधताओं और अनेकताओं का अनोखा संगम है; जिसकी अनूठी विविधता तथा अनेकता—एकरूपता और एकता की प्रतीक हैं; जिसमें विभिन्न धर्म, वर्ग, जाति तथा सम्प्रदाय के लोग रहते हैं; जिसकी संस्कृति और सभ्यता का प्रवाह सदैव सहिष्णुता तथा मानवता की ओर रहा है; जिसकी गुणगाथा, इसके अपने ही नहीं, विश्वभर के कवियों, लेखकों, साहित्यकारों और इतिहासकारों की रचनाओं का विषय बनी-वही है मेरा भारत; हमारा भारत। जितना विशाल देश, उतनी ही व्यापक समस्याएँ, अजगर की भाँति मुँह बाए, विषैले काले नाग की तरह फन फैलाए और उनसे जूझते हम भारतीय।

ये फन उठाती समस्याएँ अथवा ज्वलन्त समस्याएँ क्या हैं और इनसे जूझने की हमारी शक्ति क्या है; यदि इन दो पहलुओं को आधार बना कर विषय पर विचार न किया जाए तो विषय के साथ अन्याय करना होगा। अतः हम सर्वप्रथम इन प्रमुख समस्याओं और इनसे जूझने की शक्ति के सम्बन्ध में अपना दृष्टिकोण स्पष्ट कर देना चाहते हैं।

किसी भी राष्ट्र के सन्दर्भ में समस्याएँ मुख्यतः दो तरह की होती हैं- अपनी बनाई हुई समस्याएँ तथा बाहरी शक्तियों द्वारा थोपी गई समस्याएँ। फिर चाहें तो आप उन्हें आन्तरिक और बाहरी या राष्ट्रीय तथा अन्तर्राष्ट्रीय स्तर की समस्याओं का नाम भी दे सकते हैं। इन समस्याओं से जूझने का अर्थ है हौसले, हिम्मत और सहनशीलता से कठिनाइयों का सामना करना, अपनी क्षमताओं को बढ़ाकर उनका मुकाबला करना।

अब ऐसा समय आ गया है, जब कि हमारा देश अनेकानेक समस्याओं से जूझ रहा है। यह ठीक है कि स्वतन्त्रता प्राप्ति के पश्चात् कई समस्याओं का धीरे-धीरे हल ढूँढ निकाला गया, परन्तु फिर भी कुछ ऐसी भयावह समस्याएँ हैं, जो हमारे प्यारे भारत को अत्यधिक दुर्बल बनाती जा रही हैं। हमारा कर्त्तव्य है कि हम इन सब समस्याओं को समाप्त करने में भरसक प्रयत्न करें और अपना हार्दिक सहयोग प्रदान करें।

गिनने लगें तो आज हमारी आन्तरिक या राष्ट्रीय समस्याओं का कोई अन्त नहीं। कहीं आतंकवाद है तो कहीं अलगाववाद। कहीं गरीबी है तो कहीं महँगाई। कहीं चोरबाजारी है तो कहीं कालाबाजारी। कहीं बाढ़ है तो कहीं अकाल। कहीं रिश्वतखोरी है तो कहीं भ्रष्टाचार। अभिप्राय यह है कि आज जहाँ एक ओर रोटी से लेकर हमारी बोलचाल की भाषा तक, जीवन का हर क्षेत्र राष्ट्रीय समस्याओं का चक्रव्यूह बना हुआ है, तो दूसरी ओर अन्तर्राष्ट्रीय स्तर पर हम सीमा-विवाद, शीतयुद्ध तथा पर्यावरण जैसी समस्याओं से निरन्तर जूझ रहे हैं।

सबसे पहले हम आतंकवाद और अलगाववाद की समस्या पर विचार करें तो ज्ञात होता है कि देश के कई प्रदेशों में आतंकवाद फैला हुआ है। क्या पंजाब, क्या कश्मीर, क्या नागालैण्ड, क्या मिजोरम, क्या असम और क्या दार्जिलिंग-सर्वत्र आतंकवाद का बोलबाला है।

दूसरी समस्या है साम्प्रदायिकता की। हमारे देश में प्रायः कई धर्मावलम्बियों का निवास है। परतन्त्र भारत में अंग्रेजों की कूटनीति के कारण सभी सम्प्रदायों में फूट पड़ने लगी और आज इसी साम्प्रदायिकता के फलस्वरूप सभी एक दूसरे की हत्या करने पर तुले हुए हैं।

अयोध्या के मन्दिर और बाबरी मस्जिद की समस्या से भी हमें अब तक छुटकारा नहीं मिल पा रहा। भ्रष्टाचार, महँगाई, बेरोजगारी आदि प्रमुख राष्ट्रीय समस्याएँ तो दूर होने का नाम ही नहीं ले रहीं। परन्तु हम पूछते हैं कि जिन समस्याओं का उल्लेख हमने अभी किया, वे किस राष्ट्र में नहीं हैं? ये समस्याएँ किसी विशिष्ट समाज अथवा राष्ट्र विशेष की सीमाओं तक ही सीमित नहीं हैं; क्योंकि मानव का मानवीय मूल्यों से गिर जाना, अपने चरित्र से गिर जाना ही—समस्याओं को जन्म देता है तथा जहाँ-जहाँ मानव हैं, वहाँ-वहाँ समस्याएँ होंगी ही। अन्तर केवल इतना है कि कोई हार मानकर घुटने टेक देता है तो कोई अपनी आत्मबल की शक्ति के सहारे उन चुनौतियों का सामना करने लगता है, उनसे जूझने लगता है।

इस सम्बन्ध में यदि हम यह कहें कि अभी तक हम भारतीय भाग्यशाली रहे हैं तो कोई अतिशयोक्ति नहीं होगी। हम उस समाज के अंग हैं, हम उस राष्ट्र की इकाई हैं; जहाँ राम, कृष्ण, बुद्ध, नानक, हरिश्चन्द्र, गाँधी तथा अम्बेडकर जैसी महान् विभूतियों ने जन्म लिया। जिसे इतिहास आज भी 'सोने की चिड़िया' के नाम से जानता है, जिसके संसाधनों की पूँजी सदा से विदेशियों की आँखों में खटकती रही, उनकी ईर्ष्या का कारण बनती रही। शायद उसी का परिणाम है कि आज कहीं मन्दिर-मस्जिद के नाम पर आदमी को आदमी से गुमराह करके लड़वाया जा रहा है तो कहीं भाषा और प्रान्त के नाम पर मनुष्य के हृदय में ज़हर भरा जा रहा है। लेकिन यह हमारी जूझते रहने की शक्ति का ही परिणाम है कि इतनी समस्याएँ होने के बावजूद आज भी भारत का विश्व में अपना महत्वपूर्ण स्थान बना हुआ है, वर्ना ऐसे भी देश हैं, जहाँ समस्याएँ तो अपेक्षाकृत बहुत कम हैं, परन्तु विश्व-पटल पर आपने उनका नाम तक नहीं सुना होगा।

लेकिन हम अपनी उस जूझने की शक्ति को तो बनाए रख सकते हैं, जो मानवीय मूल्यों से मिलती है; एक दूसरे का दुःख, एक दूसरे की पीड़ा समझने से मिलती है। फिर चाहे समस्या पंजाब की हो या कश्मीर की या फिर प्राकृतिक विपत्तियों की; हमें विश्वास है कि यदि हम मानवता का मार्ग अपनाते रहें तो समस्याएँ स्वयं ही सुलझ जाएँगी—वे समस्याएँ, जो हमारी अपनी देन हैं तथा वे भी, जो हम पर बाहरी शक्तियों द्वारा थोपी जाती हैं।

अन्त में हम कह सकते हैं—पारस्परिक सौहार्द से, भाईचारे से और स्वदेश-प्रेम की भावना से इन सभी समस्याओं का समाधान किया जा सकता है।

Language Skills and Comprehension **119**

XVI. समय का सदुपयोग

संस्कृत में एक उक्ति है-

"समय एव करोति बलाबलम् ।"

अर्थात् समय ही व्यक्ति को बलवान् और निर्बल बनाता है। इसका तात्पर्य यह है कि जो व्यक्ति समय की नब्ज़ पहचान कर कार्य करता है, वह शक्तिशाली बन जाता है और जो सामने आये समय का आदर नहीं करता अथवा लापरवाही बरतता है, वह निर्बल हो जाता है।

समय सबसे बड़ी सम्पत्ति है। सम्पत्ति के बिना या धन के अभाव में व्यक्ति को कोई नहीं पूछता। अतः समय रूपी धन की मूल्यवत्ता को समझते हुए इसे कभी व्यर्थ नहीं गँवाना चाहिए। रुपये-पैसे की दौलत यदि कभी बर्बाद भी हो जाती है तो पुनः मेहनत से इस दौलत को इकट्ठा किया जा सकता है, परन्तु बहुमूल्य समय की दौलत एक बार गँवा दी जाती है तो उसका दोबारा पाना असम्भव हो जाता है। भौतिक सम्पत्ति कमाना तो मनुष्य के हाथ में है। वह चाहे जैसे-तैसे परिश्रम करके इसे एकत्रित कर सकता है, लेकिन मानव-आयु के संदर्भ में समयरूपी धन का भण्डार तो सीमित है। इसकी सीमा प्रकृति ने निश्चित की हुई है। इस सीमा को न तो हम कम कर सकते हैं और न ही अपनी इच्छा से दुगना या चौगुना कर सकते हैं।

समय की रचना एक-एक पल से होती है। जब बहुमूल्य एक-एक पल जीवन को चलाता है तो हमें उस अमूल्य पल का सदा सदुपयोग करना चाहिए, न कि दुरुपयोग। यदि हम पलों से निर्मित अपने बहुमूल्य समय को नष्ट कर देंगे तो हमारे जीवन की प्रगति रुक जायेगी। किसी एक अमूल्य क्षण को उपेक्षापूर्वक गँवा बैठना मानव की सबसे बड़ी भूल होगी। वह इस भूल से आजीवन पश्चाताप की आग में जलता रहेगा।

एक विदेशी विद्वान् का कथन है कि-

"हमारा हर दिवस एक छोटी ज़िन्दगी की भाँति है तथा हमारी सारी ज़िन्दगी उस एक दिवस की आवृत्ति मात्र है। इसलिये हर दिन को यह समझकर जिओ कि यह एक दिन हमारा सबसे आखरी दिन है।"

यह संसार कर्म की प्रधानता को सम्मुख रख कर रचा गया है। अतः हमें समय की शक्ति को पहचानते हुए अपना कर्म करते रहना चाहिए। यदि हम कर्मलीन जीवन व्यतीत करना अपना धर्म समझेंगे तो सदा कामयाब रहेंगे, अन्यथा व्यर्थ समय गँवा कर, अकर्मण्य बन कर असफलता का ही मुँह देखते रहेंगे। कर्मफल की निर्भरता समय के अधीन होती है।

जो व्यक्ति समय का सदुपयोग करते हैं, उन्हें अपने कर्मों का उचित फल अवश्य मिलता है। इसके विपरीत जिन्हें समय की उपयोगिता का बिल्कुल ध्यान नहीं रहता, वे अपने कर्मों का फल क्या प्राप्त करेंगे? समयनिष्ठता मानव जीवन के लिये सर्वोत्तम वरदान है। इस क्षणभंगुर जीवन में समयनिष्ठ व्यक्ति सफलता की सीढ़ी पर अतिशीघ्र आरोहण कर लेता है। 'बीता हुआ समय कभी नहीं लौटता' यह सोच कर मनुष्य को उसकी उपयोगिता हर पल मस्तिष्क में धारण करनी चाहिए।

XVII. महिलाओं के समान अधिकार

महिलाओं को प्रत्येक क्षेत्र में समान अधिकार देना आवश्यक है। यह एक मनोवैज्ञानिक प्रक्रिया है कि जब भी आवश्यकताओं के विषय में कोई प्रश्न उठता है तो प्रायः लोग व्यक्तिगत आवश्यकताओं को ही सीमा मान कर विचार करने लगते हैं। परन्तु ऐसा करना इस विषय में निहित समस्या के साथ सर्वथा अन्याय होगा। इस सम्बन्ध में यहाँ कुछेक तथ्यों को स्पष्ट करना आवश्यक है।

पहली बात तो यह कि हमें इस विषय को व्यक्तिगत स्तर से ऊपर उठ कर समझना है अर्थात् यह बात अपने मस्तिष्क से निकाल देनी होगी कि यदि हम पुरुष हैं तो हमें इस विषय में विरोध में ही अपने तर्क प्रस्तुत करने चाहिए या फिर यह कि क्योंकि हम महिलाएँ हैं, अतः हमें इस बात का समर्थन ही करना चाहिए।

दूसरी बात यह कि हम इस विषय पर विचार करते समय यह न भूलें कि हमें महिलाओं के लिये समान अधिकारों की आवश्यकताओं को आधुनिक परिस्थितियों के सन्दर्भ में देखना है, बदलते युग में उसकी आवश्यकताओं को समझते हुए परखना है।

तीसरी महत्त्वपूर्ण बात यह कि महिलाओं के लिये केवल समान अधिकारों की ही बात हो रही है—विशेष अधिकारों की नहीं। यद्यपि हमारे संविधान के अनुच्छेद 15 (3) के अनुसार महिलाओं और बच्चों के हित के लिये विशेष कानून बनाये जा सकते हैं और इस कथन को चुनौती देना संविधान के उन रचनाकारों को चुनौती देना होगा, जिनके मानसिक व बौद्धिक स्तर का यह परिचय है।

समान अधिकार का अर्थ है कि समानता उन अधिकारों की हो, जो पुरुषों को दिये गये हैं। यदि पुरुष को हर क्षेत्र में अधिकार प्राप्त हैं तो उसकी जननी को क्यों नहीं, जिसे कर्त्तव्य और उत्तरदायित्व का बोझ देकर उससे

समाज के उत्थान में महत्त्वपूर्ण भूमिका की अपेक्षा की जाती है। ऐसा न करके हम स्वयं के साथ ही नहीं, अपितु पूरे समाज, पूरे राष्ट्र और पूरी मानवता के साथ धोखा कर रहे हैं; अधिकारों का प्रदान करना, स्वतन्त्रता देने का ही दूसरा रूप है।

आवश्यकताएँ समय के साथ-साथ बदलती हैं, फिर चाहे वे कर्त्तव्य की हों अथवा अधिकारों की। इस बात के कई उदाहरण हमें अपने व्यक्तिगत जीवन से ही मिल सकते हैं। परन्तु उदाहरणों की आवश्यकता तब होती है, जब कथन स्वयं स्पष्ट न हो। अतः यदि हम महिलाओं को समान अधिकार देने में भी हिचकिचाएँ तो यह हमारी दुर्बलता को व्यक्त करता है। इसका तो अर्थ यही होगा कि शायद पुरुष महिला को प्रतिस्पर्धा में देख कर घबराता है, जो उसे बराबर के अधिकार देने का भी विरोध करने लग गया है।

प्रश्न केवल यह नहीं कि क्या समान अधिकार देने चाहिएँ, अपितु क्या समान अधिकार हर क्षेत्र में देना आवश्यक है? विधि के सिद्धान्तों के अनुसार कर्त्तव्य तथा अधिकार एक-दूसरे से अलग नहीं चल सकते। इसलिये यदि महिलाओं को कर्त्तव्य का बोझ दिया जाता है, जिम्मेदारी दी जाती है तो इसका पालन वे अधिकारों के बिना कर पाने में समर्थ नहीं हो सकतीं, क्योंकि कर्त्तव्य और अधिकार एक-दूसरे के पूरक हैं। एक-दूसरे के बिना अधूरा है और एक के बिना दूसरा जीवन के किसी भी क्षेत्र में वांछित परिणाम नहीं दे सकता।

वास्तविकता से, सच्चाई से मुहँ तो मोड़ा जा सकता है, पर उसे ग़लत तर्कों के आधार पर झुठलाया नहीं जा सकता। अतः नारी का जितना भी अधिक सद्भावनापूर्ण सदुपयोग हम विभिन्न कार्यक्षेत्रों में करेंगे, वह उतनी ही अधिक राष्ट्रनिर्माण के कार्यों में, समाज के उत्थान में सहायक सिद्ध होगी और यह तभी सम्भव है, जब उसे जीवन के हर क्षेत्र में यदि विशेष अधिकार नहीं तो कम से कम पुरुषों के समान अधिकार दिये जाएँ।

आज भारतीय समाज में महिलाओं का विशिष्ट स्थान है। वर्तमान काल में वे भारतीय संस्कृति की डोर सम्भालने वालों की सहयोगिनी बन चुकी हैं। यही कारण है कि अनेक भारतीय महिलाएँ देवी तथा जगमाता कहलाने की भी अधिकारिणी हैं। अतः महिलाओं को पुरुषों के समान अधिकार देने में कोई आपत्ति नहीं होनी चाहिए।

पत्र लेखन

I. पुस्तकें मँगवाने हेतु प्रकाशक को पत्र

सेवा में,
प्रबंधक महोदय
आर्य बुक डिपो
करोल बाग, दिल्ली

महोदय,

विश्वस्त सूत्रों से ज्ञात हुआ है कि आपके यहाँ ज्ञानवर्द्धक, आकर्षक व पाठ्यक्रम संबंधी सभी पुस्तकें उचित मूल्य पर मिलती हैं। हमें अपने महाविद्यालय के लिए 10,000 रुपये तक की पुस्तकें खरीदनी हैं। आप कृपया अपना सूची पत्र अविलम्ब भेजने का कष्ट करें ताकि उसको देखकर हम आवश्यक पुस्तकों के लिए माँग का आदेश दे सकें। पुस्तकों की सूची के साथ-साथ उसकी मूल्य सूची अवश्य भेजें, साथ ही खरीदी जाने वाली पुस्तकों पर कमीशन की दर भी लिखें।

धन्यवाद सहित

भवदीय

....

पता

....

....

....

....

....

फोन नं...

II. खेल-कूद संबंधी सामग्री मंगवाने हेतु डीलर को पत्र

पता

....

....

....

....

सेवा में,

प्रबधक

....

....

....

....

महोदय,

विश्वस्त सूत्रों से मिली जानकारी के द्वारा हमें पता चला है कि आपके यहाँ खेलकूद संबधी सामान उचित दर पर कमीशन काटकर मिलता है। आप कृपया खेलकूद संबंधी सामग्री की सूची एवम् कीमत सूची शीघ्रातिशीघ्र भेजने का कष्ट करें। साथ ही धन संबंधी या कोई अन्य औपचारिकता हो तो उससे भी हमें अवगत कराएं। आर्डर देने के उपरांत इस सामान को कब तक उपलब्ध करा सकेंगे, इसकी भी जानकारी दें।

धन्यवाद सहित

भवदीय

....

फोन नं. ....

ई मेल ....

III. खेल-कूद संबंधी प्रतियोगिता में भाग लेने संबंधी आवश्यक जानकारी हेतु उपकुलपति को पत्र

निखिल गुप्ता
15, सिविल लाइन्स
दिल्ली

सेवा में,
उपकुलपति महोदय
दिल्ली विश्वविद्यालय
छात्र मार्ग, दिल्ली

विषयः प्रतियोगिता में भाग लेने संबंधी आवश्यक जानकारी प्राप्त करने हेतु

महोदय,
मैं (निखिल गुप्ता) मोती लाल नेहरू महाविद्यालय का छात्र दिल्ली विश्वविद्यालय की खेलकूद संबंधी प्रतियोगिता में भाग लेना चाहता हूँ। इस संबंध में एक खिलाडी छात्र से आप क्या-क्या अपेक्षाएँ रखते हैं तथा इससे संबंधित क्या-क्या औपचारिकता निभानी पड़ती है? यदि आप इससे संबंधित तथ्यों (आवेदन की अंतिम तिथि, नियम, धन) से मुझे अवगत करा सकेंगे तो मैं आपका अत्यंत आभारी रहूँगा।
धन्यवाद

आपका कृपाकांक्षी
निखिल गुप्ता
15, सिविल लाइन्स
दिल्ली
फोन नं. ....

IV. कालेज के प्रथम वर्ष में प्रवेश पाने पर पिताजी/अभिभावक को पत्र

49–ए
पॉकेट – 3
ब्लाक – बी
सैक्टर – 18
चण्डीगढ़
तिथि ....

आदरणीय पिताजी,
सादर प्रणाम
आपके आशीर्वाद व ईश्वर की अनुकम्पा से मुझे कॉलेज में प्रवेश मिल गया है, पर यहाँ का वातावरण विद्यालय के वातावरण से बिल्कुल भिन्न है। न यहाँ पर यूनिफार्म को पहनने की अनिवार्यता है, न बैग ढोने की और न कक्षा में उपस्थित होने की। सभी छात्र अपने आप को उन्मुक्त महसूस कर रहे हैं। महाविद्यालय के परिसर में प्रवेश करते ही ऐसा महसूस होता है कि रंग-बिरंगी वेशभूषाओं का मेला-सा लगा हुआ है।

इस नये वातावरण में मैं भी समायोजित होने का प्रयास कर रहा हूँ पर साथ ही मुझे इस बात का एहसास है कि आदर्श लोक की कल्पना करने के साथ-साथ मैं यथार्थ के धरातल से अपना नाता न तोड़ूँ। फैशन की भीड़ में मैं इतना न खो जाऊँ कि मुझे अपने अस्तित्व का ज्ञान ही न रहे।

मैं यहाँ क्यों आया हूँ, मेरे भावी जीवन का उद्देश्य क्या है, यह मुझे अच्छी तरह से पता है इसलिए मैंने अभी से, अपनी एक निश्चित दिनचर्या बना ली है और उसके अनुसार चलना शुरू कर दिया है। आवश्यक पुस्तकें भी खरीद ली हैं और अतिरिक्त पुस्तकों द्वारा पढ़ने के लिए पुस्तकालय भी जाना निश्चित कर लिया है।

मैं आपकी आकांक्षाओं में खरा उतरूँ। आपके स्वप्नों को साकार करूँ इसके लिए मुझे आपके वरदहस्त की आवश्यकता है। आदरणीय माता जी, दादी जी को मेरा चरण स्पर्श कहें व नीतू को प्यार दें।

आपका कृपाकांक्षी
....

V. राष्ट्रीय स्तर क्रिकेट टीम में चुने जाने पर पिताजी को पत्र

50 ए-3 पाकेट
रोहिणी, दिल्ली
तिथि ....

आदरणीय पिताजी,
चरण स्पर्श

आपको यह जानकर हार्दिक प्रसन्नता होगी कि राष्ट्रीय स्तर पर खेलने वाली क्रिकेट की टीम का मैं सर्वसम्मति से खिलाड़ी चुन लिया गया हूँ। पिताजी, इस सफलता के पीछे आपका योगदान है। आपने विद्यालय स्तर पर होने वाली प्रतियोगिता में जो मेरा उत्साह बढ़ाया, मुझे अच्छे प्रशिक्षक से प्रशिक्षण दिलाया, यह सब उसका ही परिणाम है। मुझे अब अहसास हो रहा है बचपन में आपने जो प्रतिदिन मुझसे कसरत करवाकर मेरे शरीर को पुष्ट बनवाया है और मेरे अंदर, आत्मविश्वास, कर्मनिष्ठ और सहयोग से काम करने के जिस गुण को विकसित किया है उसके फलीभूत होने का अवसर आ गया है।

मैं अब तक आपकी व अपने गुरूओं की आकांक्षाओं पर जिस प्रकार खरा उतरा हूँ भविष्य में उसमें सफल होऊँ, इसके लिए मुझे आपके आशीर्वाद की परम आवश्यकता है।

घर में सबको यथायोग्य मेरा अभिवादन स्वीकार हो।

आपका अपना ही

....

Comprehension

I. COMPREHENSION EXERCISE

It is interesting to learn about the story of human development. Details about how humans progressed from a simple nomadic life to the present state of civilization make an exciting narrative. Historians help us to unfold this narrative by reconstructing the facts and events of the past in a systematic and scientific manner. Writing the history of modern events is comparatively easier as volumes of source material are available in libraries and museums. Official records, governmental orders, original copies of treaties and agreements, in addition to writings and manuscripts of numerous authors are at their disposal for recording events. Recording of the historical past, especially events of the pre-historic period (period for which there are no written records) is much more complex and difficult. A historian has to depend upon various sources of information such as:

a. Archaeological sources,
b. Inscriptions,
c. Numismatics,
d. Literary sources and manuscripts, and
e. Account of foreign travellers.

Answer the following questions:

Q.1. Why is writing of the modern history easy?

Q.2. What is pre-historic age?

Q.3. What do you understand by the terms (a) Numismatics, and (b) Inscriptions.

Q.4. Mention the sources which provide information on medieval history.

Q.5. Suggest the suitable title to the paragraph.

II. COMPREHENSION EXERCISE

The history can safely be divided into three periods—Ancient, Medieval and Modern. The Ancient Period started very long ago—as long as humans have lived on earth. It includes the pre-historic period, the time before we learnt how to record events. This period started many years before the birth of Jesus Christ and Christianity. Hinduism, Jainism, Buddhism, Zoroastrianism and Jewism existed much before that. The Medieval Period started from about 8th century AD and lasted till the beginning of the 18th century. Prophet Mohammad lived in this period and Islam came into being. The society, economy, polity and culture of the ancient and the medieval periods were very different from each other.

Answers/Questions:

Q.1. What does the ancient period include?

Ans. The ancient period includes the pre-historic period the time before we learnt to record events.

Q.2. Which religions existed before Christianity?

Ans. Hindusim, Jainism, Buddhism, Zorastrianism and Jewism existed before Christianity.

Q.3. When did Islam came into being?

Ans. Islam came into being in the medieval period.

Q.4. How were the ancient and medieval periods different from each other?

Ans. They were different in the form of society, economy, polity and culture.

Q.5. Give a suitable title to the paragraph.

Ans. Periodization in History.

III. COMPREHENSION EXERCISE

The application of modern science and technology to analyse and improve performance in sports is constantly thrust in. Until a few decades ago sports was viewed as the direct control of religious leaders. As the modern technology, urbanisation and economic globalisation paced up in way of life, sport has been dramatically replaced as integrated part of rapid changing society. As we marched to a new century, the application of science and technology has engulfed in all human spheres of life including sport. Participating in sport not only inculcate a strong discipline, a test for perfection and the experience of beautiful and perfect acts, but it also enhance to human growth and ensure greater stability to the global economy and polity.

Answer the following questions:

Q.1. Why is the modern science and technology constantly thrust in?

Q.2. What lead sports change into an integral part of rapid changing society?

Q.3. What happens as we march to a new century?

Q.4. What is now sports considered as?

Q.5. List out the benefits of sports.

IV. COMPREHENSION EXERCISE

From Pascal to Voltaire, the Neoclassical period is synonymous with the 'Age of Reason', 'the Enlightenment', or 'the Century of Light'. These are terms indicative of relative quintessence, the triumph of consolidation and harmony over innovation and disorder. There is some truth in these phrases, but not the whole truth. For example, although the Renaissance or the Reformation appear to be at complimentary. Opposite poles, by 1700 the tension between the two conceptions of man in a state of nature and a man in a state of grace, had softened. John Milton, writing "PARADISE REGAINED" (1671) in his old age, portrays Christ raising a demmural about the moral worth of classical pagan writers. Almost 200 years later, Mathew Arnold was to descant on these when he opposed the Hebraic to the Hellenic strand in our culture. Most important is Milton's unceasing striving to realise the condition of Christian Humanism and to unite the values implicit in Renaissance and Reformation.

Answer the following questions:

Q.1. Which is the neo-classical period?

Q.2. What does the term 'the Enlightenment' indicate?

Q.3. Why is it said that these phrases are partially true?

Q.4. What did John Milton write in 'Paradise Regained'?

Q.5. What did Milton unceasingly strive for?

V. COMPREHENSION EXERCISE

Although Rabindranath Tagore remained, a well-known and popular author in the West until the end of 1920s, interest in his work later declined. Mary Lago's critical biography of the poet suggests two possible reasons. Most English translations of his work fail to convey its true qualities. Second, many of Tagore's early poems and later works have never been translated and remain available only in Bengali. An Indian scholar, Krishna Kriplanai, says in his biography of the poet, "Tagore's main significance lies in the impulse and direction he gave to India's culture and intellectual development."

Answers/Questions:

Q.1. Name the authors of Rabindranath Tagore biography.

Ans. The authors of Rabindranath Tagore biography are Mary Lago and Krishna Kriplanai.

Q.2. What are the two possible reasons for the decline in Rabindranath Tagore's popularity?

Ans. The two possible reasons for the decline in Rabindranath's popularity are:

(a) His translations were incapable of conveying the full meaning, and

(b) Many of his works were never translated.

Q.3. What is the impact of Tagore's work on Indian culture?

Ans. He gave an impulse and direction to Indian culture.

Q.4. What are the languages in which Tagore has published his work?

Ans. The languages in which Tagore has published his work are Bengali and English.

VI. COMPREHENSION EXERCISE

The plays of Shakespeare can be compared to the legendary Akshaya Patra, the Pandavas in exile had. According to tradition, the Akshaya Patra could materialize food limitlessly. The plays of Shakespeare have triggered off a limitless publication of books in the form of criticism, condensation, translation, and so on, throughout the world. Every year many such books get published in different parts of the world. Obviously, the plays of Shakespeare form the cream of English literature. Even as interesting stories, the plays can appeal to the young readers of our country. Acquaintance with the plays of Shakespeare can touch up the relish of our youngsters for literature.

Answers/Questions:

Q.1. Shakespeare plays could be compared to what?

Ans. Shakespeare plays could be compared to the legendary Akshaya Patra, the Pandavas in exile had.

Q.2. What is the characteristic feature of Akshaya Patra?

Ans. The characteristic feature of Akshaya Patra is that it can materialize food limitlessly.

Q.3. What is the cream of English literature?

Ans. The plays of Shakespeare form the cream of English literature.

Q.4. How does the plays of Shakespeare appeal to the young readers?

Ans. The plays of Shakespeare certainly can attract our young readers towards the literature.

VII. COMPREHENSION EXERCISE

Charles John Huffham Dickens (1812-1870), generally known as Charles Dickens was born in Portsmouth. Due to financial crisis the education of Charles was totally neglected. At the age of twelve, Charles was forced to work in a blacking warehouse. The young novelist's experience of early life has gone into the making of many of his novels. Most of his novels appeared in monthly series. He has thrown light on many social evils of his time. He is known for the humour and pathos. He is a novelist of social realism. His language is an improved version of Victorian journalistic English. He is the most popular English novelist.

Answers/Questions:

Q.1. Give an appropriate title to this extract.

Ans. An appropriate title of this extract can be 'Charles Dickens and His Works'.

Q.2. What is the reason for Charles neglected education?

Ans. Low financial status of his family is the reason for Charles neglected education.

Q.3. Describe the term 'Social realism'.

Ans. 'Social realism' is the term utilized for those literary works where writer has drawn instances from day-to-day life. His works are the reflection of the society.

Q.4. Describe the language used by Charles Dickens.

Ans. The language used by Charles Dickens is an improved version of Victorian journalistic English.

VIII. COMPREHENSION EXERCISE

Archaeologists find out about the past by excavating the sites of ancient times as in buildings or settlements. They study artefacts such as tools and pottery to piece together a picture of everyday life in the past. They did not begin to search for real evidence until the late 18th and 19th centuries, when Europeans began to travel and collect curiosities from the ancient world. Evidence was easy enough to find in Greece and Rome. When this search took a hold, the first "archaeologists" began to travel to different parts of the world in search of evidence, and they made significant discoveries about early civilization. Today, archaeologists can make very accurate assessments of their finds. Without archaeologists, we would have only a very sketchy knowledge of history, and the lost cities of the ancient world would have stayed buried for ever.

Answer the following questions:

Q.1. Who are archaeologists?

Q.2. What do archaeologists do and when did they begin their work?

Q.3. What happened when the search in Greece and Rome took a hold?

Q.4. Today's archaeologists are different from the earlier ones. Comment.

IX. COMPREHENSION EXERCISE

Sports, when we talk of is perceived as something that's just related with games or physical activities but in reality is a much wider term. It takes care of games, but also has athletics, gymnastics, judo, etc. All these apart from their specific objectives has one common and highlighting objective of fitness. Fitness too is a broad term which talks of mental, physical and spiritual fitness of an individual. And now when we talk of sports and fitness, they really go hand-in-hand. Sports has biological, sociological and physiological activities which lay emphasis for an overall growth and development of an individual. It leads to good health, development of effective method of thinking, vocational preparation, worthy use of leisure time, training for citizenship and ethical and moral character building.

Answer the following questions:

Q.1. What is the general perception about sports?

Q.2. How would you explain the constituents of sports?

Q.3. What are the various aspects of fitness? Are they taken care of by sports?

Q.4. Healthy People, Fit Nation. Comment.

Q.5. Suggest a suitable title to the paragraph.

X. COMPREHENSION EXERCISE

A healthy body is the product of a healthy mind as the latter controls the body. Good health is a necessity for every human being. Physical well-being determines the quality of our life. A healthy physical body promotes and enhances spiritual and emotional well-being, which in turn helps us realize our potential, living life with zest to the fullest. Fitness and health benefits of exercise/sports are proven beyond any doubt. Sports are important to maintain public health and helps towards disease-free society. This is the reason why sports have become an integral part of the general education so as to develop a nation to its possible potential.

Answer the following questions:

Q.1. What controls our body?

Q.2. How sports help in maintaining the public health?

Q.3. Why sports have become an integral part of the general education?

Q.4. What are the advantages of a healthy physical body?

XI. COMPREHENSION EXERCISE

In the new millennium, sports has to be given a new status in our whole education system. No nation can develop to its possible potential unless the citizens of the nation are healthy and fit enough to carry out her designated work. The sole aim of physical education is the harmonious development of the child and the word 'harmonious' development means a child is fit in all respects, i.e., physically, mentally, socially adjusted and emotionally balanced. Sports is the most integral part of the general education. It includes large muscle activities to develop and control the different parts of the body through movements.

Answer the following questions:

Q.1. What has to be given importance in our new education system?

Q.2. Why a nation needs healthy citizens?

Q.3. What is the sole aim of physical education?

Q.4. What do you mean by 'harmonious development' of a child?

Chapter four

Boss Series

Sports Sciences

Q.1. What makes up proteins?
Ans. Proteins are formed from subunits called amino acids.

Q.2. Which are the three sources of water for an adult?
Ans. From liquids; in foods; and during metabolism.

Q.3. How much water is there in total body mass?
Ans. 40% to 60%.

Q.4. What is the time required to permit digestion and absorption of the pre-event meal?
Ans. Two or three hours.

Q.5. What is a measure of heat used to express the energy value of food?
Ans. A calorie or kilocalorie (kcal).

Q.6. Define energy.
Ans. Energy is defined as the ability to perform work.

Q.7. Name the six forms of energy?
Ans. Chemical, mechanical, heat, light, electric and nuclear.

Q.8. How many ATP molecules are formed in a complete breakdown of carbohydrate in skeletal muscle?
Ans. 36 ATP molecules.

Q.9. **Name two skeletal muscle fiber types?**

Ans. Slow-twitch fibers and fast-twitch fibers.

Q.10. **Which methods are used for determining the body's rate of energy expenditure?**

Ans. Direct and indirect calorimetry.

Q.11. **What is the net energy expenditure for horizontal running?**

Ans. 1 Kcal. Kg^{-1}. km^{-1}.

Q.12. **What is the optimal water temperature for most competitive swimming?**

Ans. 28°C to 30°C.

Q.13. **What is minute ventilation?**

Ans. Minute ventilation is a function of breathing rate and tidal volume.

Q.14. **What is a forced exhalation against a closed glottis?**

Ans. Valsalva maneuver.

Q.15. **Where does the cardiac rhythm initiated?**

Ans. At S-A Node.

Q.16. **What does the electrocardiogram provide?**

Ans. The electrocardiogram provides a record of the sequence of the heart's electrical events during the cardiac cycle.

Q.17. **What is cardiac output?**

Ans. Cardiac Output = Heart Rate × Stroke Volume.

Q.18. **Which theory proposes that a muscle shortens or lengthens because the protein filaments slide past each other without changing their length?**

Ans. Sliding filament theory.

Q.19. **Which mechanism process automatic muscular movements?**

Ans. Reflex arc.

Q.20. **What is the interface between the motor neuron and the muscle fiber?**

Ans. The neuromuscular junction.

Q.21. **Which hormone promotes cell division and cellular proliferation?**

Ans. Growth hormone.

Q.22. **Diminished insulin production results in which disease?**

Ans. Diabetes.

Q.23. **Which major factors affect training improvement?**

Ans. Initial fitness level; frequency of training; exercise intensity; duration of exercise; and type of training.

Q.24. **Which exercises per se contribute little to cardiovascular aerobic fitness?**

Ans. Resistance-training exercises.

Q.25. **Name the substance that can delay, suppress, or prevent the clotting of blood.**

Ans. Anticoagulant.

Q.26. **What is nearer to or at the front of the body?**

Ans. Anterior or ventral.

Q.27. **What is severe or complete loss of movement at a joint as the result of a disease process?**

Ans. Ankylosis.

Q.28. **What is the area between the diaphragm and pelvis called?**

Ans. Abdomen.

Q.29. **What is a localized collection of pus and liquefied tissue in a cavity called?**

Ans. Abscess.

Q.30. **What is fat cell called?**

Ans. Adipocyte.

Q.31. **Name the glands located superior to each kidney.**

Ans. Adrenal glands.

Q.32. What is the study of structure of body called?
Ans. Anatomy.

Q.33. Name the blood vessel that carries blood away from the heart?
Ans. Artery.

Q.34. What is the study of joints called?
Ans. Arthrology.

Q.35. What is lack of muscular coordination called?
Ans. Ataxia.

Q.36. What is atrium?
Ans. The superior chamber of the heart.

Q.37. What is neurology?
Ans. The study of the normal functioning and disorders of the nervous system.

Q.38. Define obesity.
Ans. Body weight more than 20% above a desirable standard due to excessive accumulation of fat.

Q.39. What is pathogen?
Ans. A disease-producing microbe.

Q.40. What is serum?
Ans. Blood plasma minus its clotting proteins (fibrinogen).

Q.41. What is sclerosis?
Ans. A hardening with loss of elasticity of tissues.

Q.42. Define inheritance.
Ans. The acquisition of body traits by transmission of genetic information from parents to offspring.

Q.43. What is the middle part of the small intestine called?
Ans. Jejunum.

Q.44. What is ligament?
Ans. Dense regular connective tissue that attaches bone to bone.

Q.45. Define vital capacity.
Ans. The sum of inspiratory reserve volume, tidal volume, and expiratory reserve volume.

Q.46. What is vein?
Ans. A blood vessel that conveys blood from tissues back to the heart.

Q.47. Define syndrome.
Ans. A group of signs and symptoms that occur together in a pattern that is characteristic of a particular disease.

Q.48. What is an association of organs that have a common function called?
Ans. System.

Q.49. What is spirometer?
Ans. An apparatus used to measure lung volumes and capacities.

Q.50. What is parturition?
Ans. Giving birth.

Q.51. What is genotype?
Ans. The genetic makeup of an organism.

Q.52. Which is the most abundant mineral in the body?
Ans. Calcium.

Q.53. What is BMR?
Ans. BMR (Basal Metabolic Rate) is the measurement of the metabolic rate under basal conditions.

Q.54. What are water soluble vitamins?
Ans. B vitamins and vitamin C.

Q.55. Name the two dentitions.
Ans. Deciduous and permanent.

Q.56. What does liver do?
Ans. Liver produces bile.

Q.57. What is removal of a tonsil called?
Ans. Tonsillectomy.

Q.58. What is the ability to ward off disease called?
Ans. Resistance.

Q.59. What is susceptibility?
Ans. Lack of resistance.

Q.60. What is edema?
Ans. Edema is an abnormal increase in interstitial fluid.

Q.61. What are capillaries?
Ans. Capillaries are microscopic blood vessels through which materials are exchanged between blood and tissue cells.

Q.62. What are sinusoids?
Ans. Microscopic blood vessels in liver are called sinusoids.

Q.63. What is pulse?
Ans. Pulse is the alternate expansion and elastic recoil of an artery wall with each heartbeat.

Q.64. What is normal resting pulse rate?
Ans. 70-80 beats/min.

Q.65. Which instrument is used to measure blood pressure?
Ans. Sphygmomanometer.

Q.66. What is cardiac arrest called?
Ans. Cessation of an effective heartbeat.

Q.67. What time does a complete cardiac cycle take?
Ans. 0.8 seconds.

Q.68. What is hemostasis?
Ans. Stoppage of bleeding.

Q.69. What is anemia?
Ans. Anemia is a condition in which the oxygen-carrying capacity of blood is reduced.

Q.70. What is whole blood?
Ans. Blood containing all formed elements, plasma, and plasma solutes in natural concentrations.

Q.71. What is cataract?
Ans. A common cause of blindness is a loss of transparency of the lens known as a cataract.

Q.72. What is difficulty in falling asleep called?
Ans. Insomnia.

Q.73. What is a state of deep unconsciousness from which a person cannot be aroused called?
Ans. Coma.

Q.74. What is monoplegia?
Ans. Paralysis of one limb.

Q.75. Which visceral organ has the broadest area for referred pain?
Ans. Kidneys.

Q.76. What is muscle strain?
Ans. Tearing of a muscle because of forceful impact, accompanied by bleeding and severe pain.

Q.77. What is radiographic anatomy?
Ans. Diagnostic branch of anatomy that includes the use of X-rays.

Q.78. What is formation of pus called?
Ans. Pyogenesis.

Q.79. What is Rh factor?
Ans. An inherited antigen on the surface of red blood cells in Rh^+ individuals.

Q.80. What is fibrous joint?
Ans. Bones united by fibrous tissue, allowing no movement.

Q.81. What is knee cap called?
Ans. Patella.

Q.82. Name the largest foot bone.
Ans. Calcaneus (heel bone).

Q.83. Name the most important wrist bone.
Ans. Scaphoid bone.

Q.84. Which bones form thorax?
Ans. The thoracic part of the spine with ribs and cartilages, and the sternum at the front, form the thorax.

Q.85. What is backbone called?
Ans. Vertebral column.

Q.86. What is gray matter?
Ans. Predominantly nerve cell bodies.

Q.87. What is white matter?
Ans. Predominantly nerve fibres.

Q.88. What are the main symptoms of cerebellar disease?
Ans. Jerky and uncontrolled movements, tremors and speech defects.

Q.89. What causes paralysis?
Ans. Anterior and middle cerebral vascular lesions.

Q.90. What is anosmia?
Ans. Loss of smell.

Q.91. Why do wounds of the scalp bleed profusely?
Ans. Because the dense connective tissue surrounding the vessels prevents the cut edges from contracting.

Q.92. What is voice box called?
Ans. Larynx.

Q.93. Which is the most mobile joint in the body?
Ans. Shoulder joint.

Q.94. On which artery the blood pressure is measured?
Ans. Brachial artery.

Q.95. Which organelle is commonly called the "protein factories" of the cell?
Ans. Ribosomes.

Q.96. **Name the process in which DNA makes an identical copy of itself prior to cell division.**

Ans. Replication.

Q.97. **What is an unrepaired mistake in replication?**

Ans. Mutation.

Q.98. **Which organelle contains hydrolytic enzymes?**

Ans. Lysosome.

Q.99. **What is the function of golgi apparatus?**

Ans. To pack secretory materials and forms lysosomes.

Q.100. **Name the sugar in RNA.**

Ans. Ribose.

Q.101. **Which salts make bone hard?**

Ans. Calcium phosphate and calcium carbonate.

Q.102. **Vitamin C deficiency causes which disease?**

Ans. Scurvy.

Q.103. **What makes intervertebral discs?**

Ans. Fibrocartilage.

Q.104. **Which term is synonymous with skin?**

Ans. Integument.

Q.105. **Which glands secrete sebum into the hair follicles of skin?**

Ans. Sebaceous.

Q.106. **Which muscle abducts the shoulder joint?**

Ans. Deltoid.

Q.107. **Which muscle extends the knee joint?**

Ans. Vastus lateralis.

Q.108. **Which muscle abducts and medially rotates the hip joint?**

Ans. Gluteus medius.

Q.109. **Name the flexor muscle of the shoulder joint.**

Ans. Pectoralis major.

Q.110. What is myopathy?
Ans. Any disease of the muscle.

Q.111. What is aerobic respiration?
Ans. Breakdown of glucose in the presence of oxygen to produce CO_2, H_2O, and approx. 38 ATPs.

Q.112. What is an allele?
Ans. Any one of a series of two or more different genes that may occupy the same position or locus on a specific chromosome.

Q.113. What is bilirubin?
Ans. Bile pigment derived from haemoglobin during destruction of erythrocytes.

Q.114. What is immunity?
Ans. Resistance to infectious disease and harmful substances.

Q.115. Name the red, respiratory protein of erythrocyte.
Ans. Haemoglobin.

Q.116. Name the process by which a cell swells and ruptures.
Ans. Lysis.

Q.117. What is the process of chewing called?
Ans. Mastication.

Q.118. What is cardiac cycle?
Ans. The cardiac cycle is repetitive contraction and relaxation of the heart chambers.

Q.119. What is the size of the human heart?
Ans. Size of a closed fist.

Q.120. What is the location of thyroid gland?
Ans. Just inferior to the larynx.

Q.121. What does prolactin do?
Ans. It stimulates milk production in lactating females.

Q.122. Which gland is both exocrine and endocrine?
Ans. Pancreas.

Q.123. By which gland the reproductive hormones are secreted?
Ans. Ovaries, testes, placenta, and pituitary gland.

Q.124. What is sensation?
Ans. Conscious awareness of stimuli received by sensory receptors.

Q.125. By which the taste buds are usually associated?
Ans. Papillae.

Q.126. Name four basic types of taste.
Ans. Sour, salty, bitter, and sweet.

Q.127. What is sense of smell called?
Ans. Olfaction.

Q.128. What does EEG record?
Ans. The electrical activity of the brain as alpha, beta, theta, and delta waves.

Q.129. What are synergists?
Ans. Muscles that function together to produce movement.

Q.130. What determines muscle shapes?
Ans. Primarily the arrangement of muscle fasciculi.

Q.131. Which part of skull contains the eyes?
Ans. Orbits.

Q.132. Which bone "floats" in the neck?
Ans. Hyoid bone.

Q.133. What does the vertebral column do?
Ans. Provides flexible support and protects the spinal cord.

Q.134. How many tarsal bones form the ankle?
Ans. Seven.

Q.135. What is the other name of digital bones?
Ans. Phalanges.

Q.136. Name the bones of the leg.
Ans. Tibia and fibula.

Q.137. Name the components of the integumentary system.
Ans. Skin, hair, nails, and a variety of glands.

Q.138. Which kind of sensory receptors are found in the skin?
Ans. For pain, touch, hot, cold, and pressure.

Q.139. What happens when the arrector pili muscles of the skin contract?
Ans. It causes hair to "stand on end" and produces "goose flesh".

Q.140. What determines hair colour?
Ans. Amount and kind of melanin present.

Q.141. What are the two ways in which genetic variability is increased?
Ans. Crossing-over and random assortment of chromosomes.

Q.142. What are organelles?
Ans. Organelles are subcellular structures specialized for specific functions.

Q.143. In what activities is the tongue involved?
Ans. Speech, taste, mastication and swallowing.

Q.144. Name the different kinds of teeth.
Ans. Incisors, canines, premolars and molars.

Q.145. What is the function of gallbladder?
Ans. Gallbladder stores and concentrates bile.

Q.146. What is digestion?
Ans. It is the breakdown of organic molecules into their component parts.

Q.147. What is the functional unit of kidney?
Ans. Nephron.

Q.148. Name the diploid cell resulting from the union of a sperm cell and an oocyte.
Ans. Zygote.

Q.149. What is trachea?
  Ans. Air tube extending from the larynx into the thorax where it divides to form the bronchii.

Q.150. Define death.
  Ans. Death is the loss of brain functions.

Q.151. What is scrotum?
  Ans. A two-chambered sac that contains the testes.

Q.152. What does blood typing determine?
  Ans. ABO and Rh blood groups of a blood sample.

Q.153. What is coagulation?
  Ans. Coagulation is the formation of a blood clot.

Q.154. What is buffer?
  Ans. A chemical that minimizes changes in pH.

Q.155. What is pH of blood?
  Ans. 7.4.

Q.156. Which molecule is the currency of cell?
  Ans. ATP (Adenosine Tri Phosphate).

Q.157. Which molecules are released on breakdown of food?
  Ans. NADH and $FADH_2$.

Q.158. How much energy is released on breakdown of one mole of glucose?
  Ans. 686 kcal per mole.

Q.159. Name å fat digesting enzyme.
  Ans. Lipase.

Q.160. Expand RQ.
  Ans. Respiratory Quotient.

Q.161. What kind of relationship exists between walking speed and oxygen uptake?
  Ans. Linear relation upto 3-5 km/hr and upward curve at faster speeds.

Q.162. Name the band between two amino acid units.
Ans. Peptide bond.

Q.163. Name two types of diabetes.
Ans. Diabetes mellitus and Diabetes insipidus.

Q.164. What is the primary function of carbohydrate?
Ans. To supply energy for cellular work.

Q.165. What are digested products of fats?
Ans. Fatty acids and glycerol.

Q.166. Define deamination.
Ans. Process of removal of nitrogen.

Q.167. Why do muscles fatigue after strenuous exercise?
Ans. Due to deposition of lactic acid.

Q.168. Name two techniques that are used to determine energy generated by our body.
Ans. Direct calorimetry and indirect calorimetry.

Q.169. What is stair-sprinting power test?
Ans. It is a test to measure muscular-short term power.

Q.170. Where is extra glucose stored and in which form?
Ans. Glycogen in liver.

Q.171. Why are carbohydrates called as protein sparer?
Ans. Adequate carbohydrate intake helps to preserve tissue protein.

Q.172. What is hypoglycemia?
Ans. Drop in blood glucose level.

Q.173. What are compound fats?
Ans. They are composed of a neutral fat in combination with other chemicals like phosphorus and glucose.

Q.174. Which kind of fatty acids should be incorporated in our diet?
Ans. Unsaturated fatty acid.

Q.175. What does RDA stand for?
Ans. Recommended Dietary Allowance.

Q.176. Name four fat-soluble vitamins?
Ans. A, D, E and K.

Q.177. What is the main function of vitamins?
Ans. To regulate a chain of metabolic reactions.

Q.178. How much iron is normally contained in human body?
Ans. 3-5 g.

Q.179. What are cytochromes?
Ans. The enzymes that catalyze energy transfer within mitochondria.

Q.180. What is insensible perspiration?
Ans. Water which continuously seeps from deeper tissues through the skin to body's surface.

Q.182. What is "lactovovegetarian diet".
Ans. When milk and eggs are included in a vegetarian diet.

Q.183. What is chyme?
Ans. Semi-solid paste formed after digestion.

Q.183. What is normal rate of breathing?
Ans. 15 to 18 times per minute.

Q.184. What is rate of breathing after strenuous exercise?
Ans. 20-40 times per minute.

Q.185. What is tidal volume?
Ans. Volume of air expired or inspired per breath.

Q.186. What is FVC?
Ans. Forced vital capacity (FVC) is the maximum volume expired after maximum respiration.

Q.187. How does O_2 diffuse into blood from alveoli?
Ans. Due to difference in partial pressures of gases.

Q.188. What is myoglobin?
Ans. Iron-protein compound found in skeletal and cardiac muscles.

Q.189. What is Haldane effect?
Ans. Interaction between oxygen loading and carbon dioxide release.

Q.190. In which form does CO_2 exist in blood?
Ans. As bicarbonate (HCO_3^-) ion.

Q.191. What is bradycardia?
Ans. Slowing of heart rate.

Q.192. What is tachycardia?
Ans. Acceleration of heart beat.

Q.193. How much blood is pumped from left ventricles per minute?
Ans. 5000 ml.

Q.194. Which is the largest cell of human body?
Ans. Neuron.

Q.195. Where does excitation occur during movement?
Ans. At the neuromuscular junction.

Q.196. What is "All or None" law?
Ans. It means once the neuron is excited and impulses reach the neuromuscular junction, the muscle cells always contract.

Q.197. What are different types of nerves that service spindles?
Ans. Afferent, efferent, and gamma efferent.

Q.198. What are gonads?
Ans. Primary sex organs.

Q.199. Which gland is called as a master gland?
Ans. Pituitary gland.

Q.200. What is the function of insulin?
Ans. To reduce blood sugar level.

Q.201. Name two female hormones.
Ans. Estrogen and progesterone.

Q.202. Name two different kinds of muscle action.
Ans. Concentric action, and eccentric action.

Q.203. What is muscle hyperplasia?
Ans. Increase in number of muscle cells with resistance training.

Q.204. What is muscle hypertrophy?
Ans. Increase in muscle size with the resistance training.

Q.205. Expand CRT.
Ans. Circuit Resistance Training.

Q.206. Name the vitamin used to reduce muscle soreness?
Ans. Vitamin E.

Q.207. Name the male hormones?
Ans. Testosterone.

Q.208. What is the other name of growth hormone?
Ans. Other name for growth hormone is somatotropic hormone.

Q.209. What are "Pep pills"?
Ans. Amphetamines like benzidine.

Q.210. Name a stimulant found in coffee?
Ans. Caffeine.

Q.211. Which vitamin is beneficial in aerobic exercise?
Ans. Vitamin B_{15} (Pangamic acid).

Q.212. What is other name of red blood reinfusion?
Ans. Blood doping.

Q.213. What is the centre of thermo-regulation of our body?
Ans. Hypothalamus.

Q.214. How sweating prevents overheating?
Ans. By evaporation and subsequent cooling.

Q.215. What is heat acclimatization?
Ans. Adaptive changes to improve heat tolerance.

Q.216. What is ammenorrhea?
Ans. Complete cessation of menses.

Q.217. What do we call fat that is stored below the skin?
Ans. Subcutaneous fat.

Q.218. Name the fat storage tissue.
Ans. Adipose tissue.

Q.219. What is yo-yo effect?
Ans. Futility of repeated cycles of weight loss/weight gain.

Q.220. Why is regular aerobic exercise good?
Ans. It brings favourable changes in body mass and body composition.

Q.221. Where in lung exchange of gases takes place?
Ans. In alveoli (air sacs).

Q.222. What is Adam's apple?
Ans. Voice box of males is made of protruding cartilage called Adam's apple.

Q.223. Which step is common to both aerobic and anaerobic respiration?
Ans. Glycolysis.

Q.224. How many ATPs are released per molecule of glucose in anaerobic respiration?
Ans. 2 ATPs per molecule of glucose.

Q.225. What gland is known as training school of T-lymphocytes?
Ans. Thymus.

Q.226. What is average life span of RBC?
Ans. 120 days.

Q.227. What hormones are secreted by thyroid gland that regulates carbohydrate metabolism?
Ans. Thyroxine.

Q.228. What is gland?
Ans. A specialized tissue meant for secretion of something (hormone/enzyme).

Q.229. What do endocrine glands do?
Ans. They pour in their secretions directly into the blood.

Q.230. What is ventilator?
Ans. A tube/hollow pipe that is directly inserted into trachea to facilitate respiration.

Q.231. What is epiglottis?
Ans. A cartilaginous flap that covers glottis.

Q.232. What prevents trachea from collapsing when air is not there.
Ans. Cartilagenous rings.

Q.233. What is tubectomy?
Ans. Cutting of fallopian tubes.

Q.234. Expand IUCD's.
Ans. Intra uterine contraceptive devices.

Q.235. What is the "powerhouse of cell"?
Ans. Mitochondria.

Q.236. Where does fertilization take place in human female?
Ans. In fallopian tubes.

Q.237. What is the diameter of myofibrils?
Ans. 1μ.

Q.238. What is I-band?
Ans. The lighter area on a muscle fibre is called I-band.

Q.239. What is A-band?
Ans. The darker zone of a muscle fibre is called A-band.

Q.240. What is H-zone?
Ans. Centre of A-band is a region of low optical density is called H-zone.

Q.241. What are two important constituents of actin helix structure?
Ans. Tropomyosin and troponin.

Q.242. What is T-system?
Ans. A network of tubules known as the transverse tubule system.

Q.243. What is triad?
Ans. A repeating pattern of two vesicles and T-tubules in the region of each Z-line.

Q.244. Name the enzyme that splits ATP in muscle?
Ans. Myosin ATPase.

Q.245. Which theory explains plausibly muscle action?
Ans. Sliding filament theory.

Q.246. Name the ion majorly involved in muscle contraction?
Ans. Ca^{++}.

Q.247. What is chemical composition of skeletal muscle?
Ans. It is 75% water, 20% protein and 5% inorganic salts.

Q.248. What is Node of Ranvier?
Ans. Schwann cells and mylein are interrupted every one or two mm along axon's length are called as the Nodes of Ranvier.

Q.249. What are main parts of motor neuron?
Ans. Cell body, axon and dendrites.

Q.250. What is synapse?
Ans. Interconnection of nerves.

Q.251. Name two types of receptors that monitor subconscious receptors?
Ans. Chemoreceptors and baroreceptors.

Q.252. How many pairs of peripheral nerves are there?
Ans. 31 pairs.

Q.253. How many pairs of cranial nerves are there?
Ans. 12 pairs.

Q.254. Which part of brain controls posture and co-ordination?
Ans. Cerebellum.

Q.255. Which part of brain controls memory and intelligence?
Ans. Cerebrum.

Q.256. What controls respiration?
Ans. Pons (hind-brain).

Q.257. What does medulla oblongata extend into?
Ans. Spinal cord.

Q.258. What are the four main lobes of cerebral cortex?
Ans. Frontal, temporal, parietal, and occipital.

Q.259. Name the part immediately above midbrain.
Ans. Diencephalon.

Q.260. What all does telencephalon contain?
Ans. It has two hemispheres of cerebral cortex, corpus striatum and medulla.

Q.261. What is the human neurons system made of?
Ans. CNS (central nervous system) and PNS (Periphreal nervous system).

Q.262. What makes up the brain stem?
Ans. The medulla, pons and midbrain make up the brain stem.

Q.263. What is neurilemma?
Ans. A thin membrane that covers the mylein sheath.

Q.264. What is temporal summation?
Ans. The neuron fires when many subthreshold excitatory impulses arrive in rapid succession.

Q.265. Which enzyme destroys acetyl choline?
Ans. Cholinesterase.

Q.266. What controls almost all exocrine glands?
Ans. They are under nervous control.

Q.267. What are the main parts of endocrine glands?
Ans. The endocrine system consists of:
  a. Host gland,
  b. Hormones, and
  c. Target/Receptor organ.

Q.268. Give one example of exocrine gland?
Ans. Salivary gland.

Q.269. Give an example of endocrine gland.
Ans. Pituitary gland.

Q.270. Which gland is "the master gland"?
Ans. The pituitary gland.

Q.271. What does insulin do?
Ans. Insulin brings down blood sugar level.

Q.272. What is the other name of pituitary gland?
Ans. Hypophysis.

Q.273. Name two gonadotropic hormones?
Ans. a. Follicle stimulating hormone (FSH), and
b. Lutenizing hormone (LH).

Q.274. What are the two hormones of thyroid gland?
Ans. Thyroxine (T_4), and triiodo-thyronine (T_3).

Q.275. Name two hormones of posterior pituitary.
Ans. Oxytocin and Vasopressin.

Q.276. Name the "insulin antagonist".
Ans. Glucagon.

Q.277. Name four factors that affect training improvement.
Ans. a. Initial fitness level,
b. Frequency of training,
c. Exercise intensity, and
d. Duration of exercise.

Q.278. On what factors does sweat vaporization takes place?
Ans. a. Surface exposed,
b. Temperature of surroundings, and
c. Connective air currents.

Q.279. Name the vitamins, their sources, and their deficiency diseases.

Ans.

Vitamin	Disease	Sources
Vitamin A	Night Blindness	Carrot, milk, eggs, papaya
Vitamin B	Beri-Beri	Pulses, eggs, groundnut
Vitamin B_2	Cheilosis	Liver, milk, meat
Vitamin B_6	Anaemia	Liver, milk, meat
Vitamin B_7	Pellagra	Fish, eggs
Vitamin B_{12}	Bloodlessness	Liver, eggs
Vitamin C	Scurvy	Orange, tomato, lemon
Vitamin D	Rickets	Sunlight, eggs, butter, fish oil
Vitamin E	Sterility	Green vegetable, milk, liver
Vitamin K	Delay in blood clotting	Green vegetable

Q.280. Name some of the diseases and the parts of body affected by them.

Ans.

Disease	Part of body affected	Disease	Part of body affected
AIDS	Immune system of body	Gout	Joints of bone
Arthritis	Inflammation of joints	Jaundice	Liver
Asthma	Lungs	Meningitis	Brain or spinal cord
Cataract	Eyes	Pleurisy	Pleara (inflammation of)
Conjunctivitis	Eyes	Polio	Motor neurons
Diabetes	Pancreas	Pneumonia	Lungs
Diphtheria	Throat	Pyorrhoea	Sockets of teeth
Glaucoma	Eyes	Tuberculosis	Lungs
Eczema	Skin	Typhoid	Intestine
Goitre	Front of the neck (due to enlargement of thyroid gland)	Malaria	Spleen
		Leukaemia	Blood
		Rickets	Bones

Chapter five

Boss Series

Sports and Games

Q.1. What is the size of basketball court?
Ans. A basketball court measures 29 metres long and 15 metres wide.

Q.2. What is the number of players in basketball team?
Ans. Each team consists of 5 players.

Q.3. What is weight and size of men's basketball?
Ans. The ball for men's game is 567 to 624 gms and 75 cm circumference.

Q.4. What is the weight and size of women's basketball?
Ans. Women team use a ball that weigh 510 gms (approximately) and about 74 cm in circumference.

Q.5. What is the size and weight of standard badminton racket?
Ans. The badminton racket is 26 inch long that weigh about 128 gms.

Q.6. What is the size of boxing ring?
Ans. It may measure 12 to 20 feet square platform.

Q.7. What is the weight of boxer's gloves?
Ans. The weight of boxer's gloves is 227 gms for amateur bouts and 170 gms for professional bouts

Q.8. What is the length of wickets in cricket?

Ans. The stumps stand 28 inches above the ground.

Q.9. What is the weight and size of the cricket ball?

Ans. The ball must be between 22.4 and 22.9 centimetres in circumference and must weight between 156 and 163 grams.

Q.10. What is the time duration of a football match?

Ans. The game of football is played for 90 minutes and is divided into two 45 minutes halves.

Q.11. What is the size and weight of ball for a football game?

Ans. The ball must be between 68-70 cm in circumference and weigh 410-450 grams.

Q.12. What is the field size of hockey game?

Ans. The field measures 91 metres long and 65 metres wide.

Q.13. What is the duration of hockey match?

Ans. The game is played for 70 minutes in two 35 minutes' periods.

Q.14. How many players are in kabaddi team?

Ans. Each team consists of 12 players, of which 7 are on court at a time.

Q.15. What is time period of Kabaddi match?

Ans. The game consists of two 20 minutes halves.

Q.16. What is the size of playing area of kabaddi game?

Ans. The kabaddi playing area is 12.50 metres × 10 metres divided by a line into two halves.

Q.17. What is the measurement of table tennis table?

Ans. The table tennis measurement is 9 feet long, 5 feet wide and 30 inches height.

Q.18. In which city is Olympic?

Ans. Greece.

Q.19. Who revived the modern Olympic Games?

Ans. Baron Pierre de Coubertin.

Q.20. Who has emerged as world No. 1 golf player in 2004?
Ans. Vijay Singh.

Q.21. Who has been named FIFA player of the year 2004?
Ans. Ronaldinho.

Q.22. Who won the Sir Garfield Sobers Trophy for Player of the Year Award at the first ICC Award ceremony held recently?
Ans. Rahul Dravid.

Q.23. Which was the first Asian City to host the Olympics?
Ans. Tokyo.

Q.24. With which sport is the Durand Cup associated?
Ans. Football.

Q.25. Who has won the football world cup the most number of times?
Ans. Brazil.

Q.26. Which game is also called Ping-Pong?
Ans. Table tennis.

Q.27. Which Indian athlete is nicknamed the Payyoli Express?
Ans. P.T. Usha.

Q.28. In which city were the ancient Olympics held?
Ans. Athens.

Q.29. In which sport does Anjali Vedpathak represent India?
Ans. Shooting.

Q.30. Who became 'Man of the Match' in the 2003 final world cup final?
Ans. Ricky Ponting.

Q.31. In which sport did Kamlesh Mehta and his wife Monalisa represent India?
Ans. Table Tennis.

Q.32. **Which former Indian cricketer was nick-named Tiger?**
Ans. Mansur Ali Khan Pataudi.

Q.33. **Which Indian hockey player was the first to be awarded the Helms Trophy in 1952?**
Ans. Kanwar Digvijay Singh.

Q.34. **Which Pakistani bowler has a Test highest score of 257?**
Ans. Wasim Akram.

Q.35. **Which Pakistani bowler made his debut with Sachin Tendulkar?**
Ans. Waqar Younis.

Q.36. **In which cricket World Cup did Roger Binny take the most number of wickets?**
Ans. 1983.

Q.37. **Who bowled the fastest ball in the 2003 World Cup?**
Ans. Shoaib Akhtar.

Q.38. **Which country won the women's hockey world cup three times in a row between 1983 and 1990?**
Ans. The Netherlands.

Q.39. **The Davis Cup in tennis first originated as a competition between which two teams?**
Ans. U.S.A. and Great Britain.

Q.40. **The Black Brothers hail from which country?**
Ans. Zimbabwe.

Q.41. **The site of which Grand Slam event was originally on Worple Road?**
Ans. Wimbledon.

Q.42. **Who was the other finalists in Davis Cup Final in 1974 apart from India?**
Ans. South Africa.

Q.43. Which former player and current coach's autobiography is called Winning Ugly?

Ans. Brad Gilbert.

Q.44. Who was the first black tennis player to win a US Open singles championship?

Ans. Althea Gibson.

Q.45. Which player won the 1999 Wimbledon Ladies Single tennis title?

Ans. Lindsay Davenport.

Q.46. Who or what is 'Rebound Ace'?

Ans. An artificial surface for playing tennis.

Q.47. Leander Paes' mother represented India in which sport?

Ans. Basketball.

Q.48. Who was Vijay Amritraj's doubles partner for most of his carrier?

Ans. Anand Amritraj.

Q.49. What is the full form of B.A.T.?

Ans. Britannia Amritraj Tennis Academy.

Q.50. Which player's father was arrested, convicted and jailed for tax evasion on his daughter's earings?

Ans. Steffi Graf.

Q.51. Who or what were Jimbo and Mac?

Ans. Jimmy Connors and John McEnroe.

Q.52. Which is the oldest of the tennis Grand Slams?

Ans. Wimbledon.

Q.53. Which Indian player became the head of the ATP (Association of Tennis Professionals)?

Ans. Vijay Amritraj.

Q.54. Which tournament is played in a stadium named after a world war I flying ace?

Ans. The French Open.

Q.55. Which James Bond movie did Vijay Amritraj act in?
Ans. Octopussy.

Q.56. Who won the 1990 Wimbledon women's singles title?
Ans. Martina Navratilova.

Q.57. Who won the tennis gold medal at the 1996 Atlanta Olympic Games?
Ans. Andre Agassi

Q.58. Which tennis player's father represented Iran in boxing at the Olympics?
Ans. Andre Agassi.

Q.59. Who, in 1990 became the youngest man to win the US Open singles title?
Ans. Pete Sampras.

Q.60. Who was the first Indian tennis player to reach a Wimbledon singles semifinal?
Ans. Ramanathan Krishnan.

Q.61. Name the tennis player responsible for the T-shirt with the alligator logo.
Ans. Rene Lacoste.

Q.62. Name the person who holds the record for winning the greatest number of Wimbledon tournaments—singles, doubles and mixed doubles.
Ans. Billie Jean King.

Q.63. Name the first Asian ever to win a Junior Wimbledon title.
Ans. Ramanathan Krishnan.

Q.64. Who finally defeated Leander Paes in his bronze medal winning run at the 1996 Olympics?
Ans. Andre Agassi.

Q.65. Who is Melanie Molitor's well-known daughter?
Ans. Martina Hingis.

Q.66. What is the claim to fame of one Sirdar Nihal Singh?
Ans. The first Indian to play at Wimbledon.

Q.67. When did India first play the Davis Cup?
Ans. 1921.

Q.68. Who was the player who cried on the shoulders of royalty after gifting away a Wimbledon final to Steffi Graf?
Ans. Jana Novotna.

Q.69. In the 1970s who were the ABCs of tennis?
Ans. Amritraj-Borg-Connors.

Q.70. Who are the only father-son Indian pair to win Junior Wimbledon?
Ans. The Krishnans.

Q.71. Where was tennis as an Olympic sport revived?
Ans. The Seoul Olympics.

Q.72. Who is nicknamed 'the Ghost' from Ostrava?
Ans. Ivan Lendl.

Q.73. The tennis player, Sebastian Lareau, is from which country?
Ans. Canada.

Q.74. In 1971, who became the youngest player to reach the semifinals of the US Championship?
Ans. Chris Evert.

Q.75. Who retired after the 1994 season, having won 167 titles in tennis in all?
Ans. Martina Navratilova.

Q.76. In Japan, what is the Jubilo Iwata?
Ans. A football team.

Q.77. Name the first Asian city to have hosted the Olympics?
Ans. Tokyo.

Q.78. Name the Korean martial art which was first introduced as an exhibition sport at the 1988 Seoul Olympics.

Ans. Taekwando.

Q.79. In which discipline was the action hero Bruce Lee, an expert?

Ans. Kung Fu.

Q.80. The name of which Japanese martial art literally means 'Empty Hand'?

Ans. Karate.

Q.81. 1972 bronze medallist, Ashok Kumar, is the son of which legendary Indian Olympian?

Ans. Dhyan Chand.

Q.82. What is the stick used in snooker called?

Ans. A cue.

Q.83. How many decks of cards in Poker played with?

Ans. One.

Q.84. Which chess piece can move one square at a time in any direction?

Ans. The king.

Q.85. Bermuda Bowls is the world championship in which card game?

Ans. Bridge.

Q.86. What card game is played with 108 cards?

Ans. Canasta.

Q.87. In an international game of Judo, what is the 'Shiagio'?

Ans. The contest area.

Q.88. What were the precursors of modern boxing gloves called?

Ans. Mufflers.

Q.89. **Who was the captain of the Sri Lankan team that won the 1996 World Cup cricket tournament?**
Ans. Arjuna Ranatunga.

Q.90. **In 1990, which heavy weight boxer defeated Mike Tyson?**
Ans. James Douglas.

Q.91. **In 2001 what technical change was made to the table tennis ball?**
Ans. Diameter was increased by 2 mm.

Q.92. **Which Indian female badminton player was once suspended by the IBF for taking a banned substance?**
Ans. Aparna Popat.

Q.93. **Which South African cricketer is nicknamed Zulu?**
Ans. Lance Klusener.

Q.94. **Who was the captain of the first South African cricket team to visit India after the lifting of the ban?**
Ans. Clive Rice.

Q.95. **In tennis where is the French Open played?**
Ans. Roland Garros.

Q.96. **Mike Tyson bit off a part of the ear of which boxer during a boxing match?**
Ans. Evander Holyfield.

Q.97. **What is the name of Muhammed Ali's daughter, who is also a boxer?**
Ans. Laila Ali.

Q.98. **In which sport would you use a puck?**
Ans. Ice hockey.

Q.99. **In which sport would you find matadors and picadors?**
Ans. Bullfighting.

Q.100. The Chinese game Tsu Chu and the Japanese game kemari are ancient forerunners of which modern day ball game?

Ans. Football.

Q.101. Springboard and platform are the two major disciplines of which aquatic event?

Ans. Diving.

Q.102. The rugby team of which country is named All Blacks?

Ans. New Zealand.

Q.103. The Rangaswamy Cup is the Indian national championship for which sport?

Ans. Hockey.

Q.104. The America's Cup is one of the most prestigious events in which sport?

Ans. Yachting.

Q.105. What is the basic idea of hopscotch?

Ans. Not treading on the lines.

Q.106. In which game can you for a white slam?

Ans. Carrom.

Q.107. Which flamboyant woman athlete and world record holder died of a heart attack in 1999?

Ans. Florence Griffith Joyner.

Q.108. With which racquet sport would you associate the terms 'Service Box' and 'Tin'?

Ans. Squash.

Q.109. In India Khel Ratna Award is named after which former Prime Minister?

Ans. Rajiv Gandhi.

Q.110. US Olympic Champion Jin Thorpe was forced is give up his Olympic medals for having played as a professional in which sport?

Ans. Baseball.

Q.111. Who made the first ever 8 metre long jump?
Ans. Jesse Ovens.

Q.112. If Mohammed Ali is 'The Greatest', 'who is 'The Great One'?
Ans. Wayne Gretzky.

Q.113. Which game when freely translated from Latin means 'I play'?
Ans. Ludo.

Q.114. The Victor Chandler world championship is held in which sport?
Ans. Billiards.

Q.115. In cricket, who or what is a Bosie?
Ans. A googly.

Q.116. Which cricket trophy in India is named after a nephew of Ranjit Singhji?
Ans. The Duleep Trophy.

Q.117. Beating the Field is the autobiography of which cricketer?
Ans. Brian Lara.

Q.118. Brazilian Jose Ramirez Barreto plays for which Indian football club?
Ans. Mohun Bagan.

Q.119. At which Olympics was the Olympic flag introduced?
Ans. Antwerp, 1920.

Q.120. Where is the Queen's Park Oval stadium situated?
Ans. Port of Spain.

Q.121. 'Being Myself', is the autobiography of which woman tennis legend?
Ans. Martina Navratilova.

Q.122. Which actress was once married to Andre Agassi?
Ans. Brooke Shields.

Q.123. Who won the women's title of the Commonwealth Chess Championship 2003?

Ans. Vijayalakshmi.

Q.124. Who won the men's title of the Commonwealth Chess Championship 2003?

Ans. Grandmaster Dibyendu Barua.

Q.125. Who was declared 'Man of the Match' in the LG Cup 2002 won by India?

Ans. Baichung Bhutia.

Q.126. Which team won the Durand Cup finals played in New Delhi in 2003?

Ans. East Bengal.

Q.127. Which team registered its maiden triumph in the Federation Cup in 2003?

Ans. Mahindra United (Mumbai).

Q.128. Which is India's largest indoor stadium?

Ans. Indira Gandhi Indoor Stadium, New Delhi.

Q.129. Which is India's largest stadium?

Ans. Yuba Bharti Stadium, Kolkata.

Q.130. Who is named as 'Wisden's Cricketer'?

Ans. Gavaskar.

Q.131. Sports goods are mainly manufactured in which part of India?

Ans. Jalandhar.

Q.132. Who said 'Play the game in the spirit of game'.

Ans. Pt. J.L. Nehru.

Q.133. With which game is the name of Syed Modi associated?

Ans. Badminton.

Q.134. Dhyan Chand's name is associated with which game?

Ans. Hockey.

Q.135. Swaythling Cup is associated with which game?
Ans. Table Tennis.

Q.136. How many players are there on each side in a women's basketball team?
Ans. Six.

Q.137. What is the duration of a normal one-half of a hockey match?
Ans. 35 min.

Q.138. Dronacharya award is associated with whom?
Ans. Sports coaches.

Q.139. What was the former name of Reliance Cup?
Ans. Prudential Cup.

Q.140. With which game is the Aga Khan Cup associated?
Ans. Hockey.

Q.141. Which game is Scindia Gold Cup associated with?
Ans. Hockey.

Q.142. Which game is Rajkumari Challenge Cup associated with?
Ans. Table Tennis (Junior Girls).

Q.143. When was Indian Olympic Council established and who was its first President?
Ans. 1924, Sir J.J. Tata.

Q.144. When did India officially participate in the Olympics?
Ans. 1920.

Q.145. What were Commonwealth Games originally called?
Ans. British Empire Games.

Q.146. What is the time interval between the two Commonwealth Games festivals?
Ans. Four years.

Q.147. When and where were the first SAF games held?
Ans. 1984, Kathmandu.

Q.148. What is the motto of SAF games?
Ans. Peace, Prosperity and Progress.

Q.149. What was the individual Indian achievement in shooting in Olympics in 2004?
Ans. Rajyavardhan Singh bagged silver medal.

Q.150. Where is the 2005 National Swimming Championship scheduled?
Ans. Kerala.

Q.151. What will be the mascot of 2010 Commonwealth Games to be held in Delhi?
Ans. Tiger.

I. LIST OF SPORTS

Athletics
Track and field athletics.
- Jumping
  - Triple jump
  - Long jump
  - High jump
  - Pole vault
- Running
  - Sprints
  - Middle distance
  - Long distance
  - Relay races
  - Hurdling
  - Steeplechase
- Throwing
  - Discus
  - Hammer throw
  - Horseshoe
  - Javelin
  - Atlatl

- Shot put
- Walking

Animal Sports: Sports in which animals play a role
- Bull fighting
- Camel racing
- Cockfighting
- Pigeon sport
- Equestrianism:
  - Quarterhorse racing
  - Steeplechase
  - Equestrianism
  - Thoroughbred racing
  - Harness racing
  - Polo
  - Buzkashi
- Dog sports

Combat Sports: Generally sports in which athletes fight or combat each other, usually one-on-one
- Aikido
- Ba Gua
- Boxing
- Brazilian jiu jitsu
- Capoeira
- Fencing
- Hapkido
- Iaido
- Judo
- Ju-jitsu
- Karate
- Kempo
- Kendo
- Kung-fu
- Mixed martial arts
- Muay Thai
- Naginata-do
- Pencak Silat
- Sambo
- Sumo

- Taekwondo
- Tai Chi Chuan
- Tang Soo Do
- Wing Chun
- Wrestling
- Wushu
- Yağli Güreş

Cycling: Sports using bicycles or unicycles
- Bicycle polo
- BMX
- Cycloball
- Cyclocross
- Mountain bicycling
- Mountain unicycling
- Road cycling
- Track cycling
- Triathlon
- Unicycle trials

Extreme Sports
- Adventure racing
- BASE jumping
- Body boarding
- Bungee jumping
- Cheerleading
- Motorcross
- Parkour
- Rock climbing
- Skateboarding
- Snowboarding
- Wakeboarding
- Surfing

Gymnastics Sports
- Artistic gymnastics
- Rhythmic gymnastics
- Sports acrobatics
- Sports aerobics
- Trampolining

Motorised Sports: Sports based on motorised transportation
- Air racing
- Auto racing
- Karting
- Motorboat racing
- Motorcycle racing

Outdoor Sports: Sports not based on a specific field
- Aerobatics
- Aeromodelling
- Ballooning
- Caving
- Casting
- Canyoning
- Fell running
- Flying disc
- Gliding
- Hang gliding
- Mountaineering
- Orienteering
- Parachuting
- Paragliding
- Scuba diving
- Skydiving
- Sled-dog sports
- Sport fishing
- Surfing
- Zorbing

Power Sports: Sports mainly based on sheer power
- Bodybuilding
- Dwarf throwing
- Powerlifting
- Tug of war
- Weightlifting
- Zurkhaneh

Racket sports: Sports where players use rackets to hit a ball or other object
- Badminton
- Paddleball

- Racquetball
- Racquets
- Real tennis
- Soft tennis
- Squash
- Squash tennis
- Stické
- Table tennis
- Tennis

Skating: Sports in which skates are used
- Artistic roller skating
- Figure skating
- Ice hockey
- Inline speed skating
- Rink hockey
- Roller derby
- Roller hockey
- Roller skating, Inline skating
- Roller speed skating
- Short track speed skating
- Skateboarding
- Speed skating
- Synchronized skating

Skiing/Snowsports: Sports in which skis or snowboards are used
- Alpine skiing (also known as *Downhill skiing*)
- Backcountry skiing (also known as *Off Piste skiing*)
- Biathlon
- Cross country skiing (together with ski jumping and nordic combined also known as *Nordic skiing*)
- Firngleiten
- Freestyle skiing
- Grass skiing
- Nordic combined
- Roller skiing
- Skibob
- Ski flying
- Skijoring
- Ski jumping

- Ski touring
- Speed skiing
- Telemark skiing
- Snowboarding
- Freestyle snowboarding
- Extreme snowboarding

Sleighing: Sports that use sleighs
- Bobsleigh
- Land luge (also known as street luge and road luge)
- Luge
- Skeleton
- Wok racing

Sports Entertainment
- Professional wrestling

Target sports: Sports where the main objective is to hit a certain target
- Archery
  - Kyudo
- Atlatl
- Billiard sports
  - Billiards
  - Bar billiards
  - Carambole billiard
  - Pool
  - Snooker
  - Trick shot snooker
- Bocce
- Boccia
- Bowling
- Croquet
- Curling
- Darts
- Golf
- Disc golf
- Speed golf
- Golfcross
- Horseshoe throwing
- Laser tag

- Lawn bowls
- Marbles
- Pall mall
- Pelota
- Petanque
- Shooting
- Skittles
- Trugo

Team Sports: Sports that involve teams
- Airsoft
- American football
- Australian rules football
- Bandy
- Baseball
- Basketball
- Basque pelota
- Broomball
- Camogie
- Canadian football
- Canoe polo
- Cricket
- Curling
- Eton wall game
- Faustball
- Floorball
- Football (soccer)
- Futsal
- Gaelic football
- Goalball
- Handball
- Field hockey
- Hornusser
- Hurling
- Ice hockey
- Kabaddi
- Korfball
- Lacrosse
- Mesoamerican ballgame
- Netball

- Paintball
- Petanque
- Polo
- Roller hockey
- Rounders
- Royal shrovetide football
- Rugby
- Scuffleball
- Sepak Takraw
- Shinty
- Skittles
- Softball
- Tchoukball
- Throwball
- Ultimate frisbee
- Volleyball
- Water polo

Mind Sports: Sports that require little or no physical abilities
- Bridge
- Chess
- Checkers (draughts)
- Poker
- Go
- Scrabble
- Shogi
- Heksup
- Dominoes

Water Sports: Sports that are played in, under or near the water

In the Water
- Swimming.
- Triathlon is usually a combination of swimming, cycling and running.
- Modern pentathlon includes epee fencing, pistol shooting, swimming, a show jumping course on horseback, and a cross-country run.
- Rescue swimming is swimming with the goal to rescue other swimmers or the practice thereof.

- Surf lifesaving is a competitive sport which evolved from the training activities of lifeguards at Australian surf beaches.
- Water polo is a team ball sport played in water.
- Synchronized swimming.
- Fin swimming.
- Water aerobics.
- Water gymnastics.
- Snorkeling.
- Diving off springboards or off platforms.
- Synchronized diving.

Under Water
- Diving under water.
- Scuba diving.
- Free-diving.
- Apnea.
- Underwater rugby.
- Underwater hockey.
- Underwater photography.

Near the Water
- Boating.
- Bodyboarding.
- Canoeing.
- Canoe polo.
- Dragon boat racing.
- Fishing.
- Hydroplane racing.
- Jet sprint boat racing.
- Kayaking.
- Kite surfing on flat water using a kite for propulsion.
- Motor boating.
- Offshore powerboat racing.
- Parasailing where a person is towed behind a vehicle (usually a boat) while attached to a parachute.
- Sailing.

II. LIST OF COUNTRIES' NATIONAL PASTIMES

- Afghanistan—Buzkashi.
- Albania—Football.
- Argentina—Football with Rugby Union and Polo.
- Australia—Cricket is the official summer sport, Rugby League is the official winter sport in the northern states (ACT, New South Wales and Queensland) and Australian Rules Football is the official winter sport in the other states and the Northern Territory.
- Austria—Alpine skiing.
- Barbados—Cricket.
- Belgium—Cycling is the most popular sport in Belgium. During winter a variant of cycling called Cyclocross ("Veldrijden") is the pastime for most Belgians (certainly in Flanders), Belgium dominates this sport totally. Footbal is also quite popular.
- Bermuda—Cricket.
- Bhutan—Archery.
- Brazil—Football is considered the national obsession, and volleyball also has a large number of participants.
- Canada—Lacrosse is the official summer sport and ice hockey is the official winter sport, but hockey is by far the sport most closely followed, and most closely linked to national pride. Designating lacrosse as an official sport is more of a nod to history that a reflection of the present-day situation: Sports like baseball, Canadian football (but probably also American football), soccer, golf, tennis are all much more popular. Canada is also the world's dominant force in the sport of Curling.
- China—Table tennis.
- Colombia—Tejo is the traditional sport, as is bullfighting, but football (soccer) is the main attraction, followed by baseball and basketball.
- Cuba—Baseball.
- Czech Republic—Ice hockey and football are close in popularity.
- Denmark—Football.
- Dominican Republic—Baseball.
- Estonia—Basketball.
- England—Football (soccer) in winter, cricket in summer; rugby union and rugby league also attract large crowds.
- Fiji—Rugby union (particularly Sevens).

- Finland—Pesäpallo, Ice Hockey.
- France—Football, but rugby union is popular in the south. Basketball is also played. Cycling is also very widely followed.
- Gambia—Wrestling.
- Germany—Football, but American football is also played (it is home to the German Football League, and five of the six teams in NFL Europe).
- Greece—Football is most popular, with basketball and volleyball right behind.
- Guyana—Cricket.
- Haiti—Football.
- Hong Kong—Dragon boat racing.
- Iceland—Glima.
- India—Field hockey is the official sport (winners of 8 Olympic Golds), but cricket is the most popular (winners of 1983 World Cup).
- Iran—Wrestling.
- Ireland—Hurling and Gaelic football.
- Israel—Football and basketball.
- Italy—The traditional sport is bocce, but football is the national passion. Basketball is also highly popular, and winter sports are followed mostly in the north.
- Jamaica—Cricket and football.
- Japan—Sumo wrestling is traditionally viewed as Japan's national sport, but baseball is today more popular, and football is rapidly increasing in popularity. Rugby union also has a substantial following.
- Korea—Taekwondo is traditional, baseball is highly popular, but StarCraft, which is actually a computer game, has sometimes sarcastically been referred to as the national sport. South Korea is also a major force in women's golf.
- Latvia—Ice hockey.
- Lithuania—Basketball.
- Mexico—Charreria is traditional, but football is most popular today, with baseball also widely played and followed.
- Mongolia—Wrestling and archery.
- Nauru—Australian rules football.

- Netherlands—Football has the largest following, but cycling and ice skating are seen as traditional sports; volleyball, baseball (known locally as *honkbal*) and field hockey are also played.
- New Zealand—Rugby union is the most widely followed and most closely linked to national pride (Rugby League not being vary far behind), although more children today play soccer. Australian Rules Football is also gaining a stronghold here. Netball is one of the most popular sports among girls and young women, and men have organised some teams of their own. Cricket is played during summer.
- Nicaragua—Baseball.
- Nigeria—Football.
- Norway—Skiing, both Nordic and Alpine.
- Pakistan—Field hockey is the official sport (winners of the Gold in 1971, 1978, 1982 and 1994), but cricket is the most popular (winners of the World Cup in 1992).
- Papua New Guinea—Rugby league.
- Philippines—Basketball.
- Poland—Football.
- Portugal—Football.
- Puerto Rico—Baseball.
- Romania—Oina is the traditional sport, but football is much more popular. Rugby also has a fairly decent stronghold.
- Russia—Football, Ice Hockey, Sambo.
- Samoa—Rugby union.
  Note: In American Samoa, American football is more popular.
- Saudi Arabia—Falconry and horse racing are traditional, but football draws the largest number of spectators.
- Scotland—Native sport is Shinty, but football attracts much larger crowds. It was also the birthplace of golf, which is more often associated with Scotland than anywhere else.
- Solvenia—Alpine skiing.
- Soviet Union—Chess, Ice Hockey.
- South Africa—Football has historically been most popular with blacks, rugby union with Afrikaners, and cricket with British-descended whites.
- Spain—Bull fighting is traditional, but football is the most popular.
- Switzerland—Hornussen, a traditional game, is popular in rural

Switzerland, although football is most popular overall, and ice hockey is rising in popularity.

- Sweden—Football and ice hockey are almost equally popular.
- Taiwan—Baseball.
- Thailand—Muay Thai.
- Tonga—Rugby union.
- Turkey—Yağli Güreş (Oil wrestling) is traditional, but football is the most popular.
- United Arab Emirates—Camel racing is traditional, but football is the most popular.
- United States—Baseball is generally named as "the American national pastime", but American football presently has the largest number of viewers, with the NASCAR (stock car racing), long popular in the southeastern states, rapidly becoming popular nationwide. Basketball is popular among the young, urban population. Football, known as Soccer in the U.S., is popular with the young, suburban population. The rise of soccer's popularity with children in suburbs have created a policitcal demographic known as the "Soccer mom". Ice Hockey was once very popular in the Northeast, Midwest as well as with Southeastern immigrants from those regions and Canada. However, the popularity of Ice Hockey appears to be waning in recent years.
- Uzbekistan—Kurash.
- Venezuela—Baseball is the most popular, with football is close second thanks to Colombian, Portuguese and Italian immigrants.
- Wales—Rugby union (although there are more football teams and it is watched by more people.

III. CUPS AND TROPHIES ASSOCIATED WITH VARIOUS COMPETITIONS

1. **Archery:** Federation Cup.
2. **Badminton:** Thomas Cup (Men), Uber Cup (Women), Yonex Cup.
3. **Basketball:** Federation Cup.
4. **Chess:** Khaitan Cup, Limca Trophy, World Cup.
5. **Cricket:** Ashes, Asia Cup, World Cup, Deodhar Trophy, C.K. Nayudu Trophy, Duleep Trophy, Vizzy Trophy, Wills Trophy.
6. **Football:** Airline Cup, Durand Cup, DCM Cup, Santosh Trophy, World Cup.

7. **Hockey:** Agha Khan Cup, Dhyan Chand Trophy, World Cup, Modi Gold Cup, Shriram Trophy.
8. **Kabaddi:** Federation Cup.
9. **Kho-Kho:** Federation Cup
10. **Lawn Tennis:** Champions Cup, Ghafar Cup, Wimbledon Trophy, Grand Prix, Davis Cup.
11. **Golf:** Ryder Cup, Walker Cup, Canda Cup, L.G. Fashion Open Trophy.
12. **Billiard:** Goldflake Trophy, Thomas Cup.

IV. IMPORTANT TERMS ASSOCIATED WITH MAJOR GAMES

1. **Badminton:** Duce, Drop, Love all, Smash.
2. **Basketball:** Basket, Blocking, Dribbling.
3. **Billiards:** Cannon, Cue, Pot, Scratch.
4. **Boxing:** Bandit Punch, Cut, Defence Hook, Knockout.
5. **Chess:** Bishop, Castle, Checkmate, Stalemate.
6. **Cricket:** Caught, Drive, Crease, Duck, Hat-trick, Hitwicket Stumped, Runout, Silly point.
7. **Football:** Corner kick, Penalty, Off side.
8. **Hockey:** Bully, Dribble, Scoop, Tie-breaker, Sudden death.
9. **Horse Riding:** Jockey, Punter.
10. **Swimming:** Breast-stroke, Crawl, Butter-fly, Free-style.
11. **Tennis:** Deuce, Volley, Smash, Drop.
12. **Volleyball:** Blocking, Service, Spiking, Holding.

V. SPORTS AWARDS AND SCHEMES

ARJUNA AWARDS

The Arjuna Award was instituted in 1961. According to recently revised Scheme of Arjuna Awards for outstanding performance in sports and games, for eligibility to the Award, a sportsperson would have had not only good performance consistently for the previous three years at the international level with excellence for the year for which the Award is recommended but also should have shown qualities of leadership, sportsmanship and a sense of discipline. The Awardee is given a statuette, a scroll of honour, ceremonial dress and a cash award of rupees three lakh.

From the year 2001, the award is being given only in disciplines falling under the following categories: (a) *Olympic Games/Asian Games/ Commonwealth Games/World Cup/World Championship disciplines and cricket;* (b) *Indigenous Games;* and (c) *Sports for physically challenged.*

RAJIV GANDHI KHEL RATNA AWARD

The Rajiv Gandhi Khel Ratna Award was instituted by the Government in 1991-92 for most spectacular and outstanding performance in the field of sports by a sportsperson/team in a year. The award, the only one given under the scheme, carries a medal, a scroll of honour and a cash prize of rupees five lakh.

DRONACHARYA AWARD

The Dronacharya Award, instituted in 1985, honours eminent coaches who have successfully trained sportspersons or teams and enabled them to achieve outstanding results in international competitions. The awardee is given a statuette of Guru Dronacharya, a scroll of honour, ceremonial dress and a cash prize of rupees three lakh.

DHYAN CHAND AWARD FOR LIFETIME ACHIEVEMENT IN SPORT AND GAMES

Dhyan Chand Award for Lifetime Achievement in Sport and Games has been instituted from the year 2002 to honour those sportspersons who have contributed to sports by their performance and continue to contribute to promotion of sports even after their retirement from active sporting career. The award carries a cash award of Rs. 1.50 lakh, a plaque and a scroll of honour.

MAULANA ABUL KALAM AZAD (MAKA) TROPHY

Inter-University Tournaments are an integral and important part of games and sports in universities and colleges. The top overall performing university in the Inter-University Tournaments is given the Maulana Abul Kalam Azad (MAKA) Trophy, which is a rolling trophy. A small replica of the MAKA Trophy is also awarded for retention by the university. In addition, the university also gets a cash prize of Rs. two lakh. The second and third best universities also receive cash awards amounting to Rs one lakh and Rs. fifty thousand respectively.

SPORTS FUND FOR PENSION TO MERITORIOUS SPORTSPERSONS

This scheme was launched in the year 1994. Under this scheme pension is given to a meritorious sportsperson after he/she attain the age of 30 years for his/her lifetime. The scheme is being operated through Life Insurance Corporation of India. The scheme has recently been revised by enhancing the rates of pensions. Besides, new categories of pension have also been added to the scheme. Pensions will now be given at the following rates:

a. Medallists at the Olympic Games	Rs 5,000 p.m.
b. Gold medallists at the World Cups/ World Championships in Olympic and Asian Games disciplines	Rs 4,000 p.m.
c. Silver and Bronze medallists of the World Cups/World Championships in Olympic and Asian Games disciplines	Rs 3,500 p.m.
d. Gold medallists of the Asian/ Commonwealth Games	Rs 3,500 p.m.
e. Silver and Bronze medallists of Asian/ Commonwealth Games	Rs 3,000 p.m.
f. Gold medallists of Para-Olympic Games	Rs. 2,500 p.m.
g. Silver medallists of Para-Olympic Games	Rs. 2,000 p.m.
h. Bronze medallists of Para-Olympic Games	Rs. 1,500 p.m.

VI. SPORTS ACHIEVEMENTS AT INTERNATIONAL-LEVEL COMPETITIONS IN 2004 BY INDIANS

India's performance in the Athens Olympic Games (13-29 August 2004) has been satisfactory. Major R.V.S. Rathore won an individual Silver Medal in Double Trap (Men's Shooting). In addition, two other shooters, Ms Suma Shirur and Abhinav Bindra reached the finals and finished eighth and seventh respectively. The Indian women's 4 × 400 metres relay team broke the existing national record to reach the finals. Ms Anju Bobby George also broke her own national record to finish sixth in the long jump for women. Sh K.M. Binu also broke the national record in men's 400 metres race to reach the semi-finals.

The Indian duo of Leander Paes and Mahesh Bhupati reached the semi-finals in tennis but narrowly lost the bronze medal play-off. In weightlifting, Ms Kunjarani Devi secured the 4th position in her weight category.

Major Sporting Events Held During the Year 2004 and Performance of Indian Teams

(a) The 9th SAF Games were held at Islamabad, Pakistan from 29 March to 7 April 2004; (b) Indian Sr. Men's team participated in Rashid International Volleyball Tournament held at Dubai from 30 July to 6 August 2004 and won a bronze medal; (c) Indian Swimming team participated in the 6th Asia-Pacific Water Polo Tournament held from 12-16 August 2004 and secured third position.

On the occasion of National Sports Day-2004, a 'Run for Sports' was organized for the first time from Major Dhyan Chand National Stadium, New Delhi on 29 August 2004.

VII. SPORTS AWARDS WON BY INDIVIDUALS

RAJIV GANDHI KHEL RATNA AWARD FOR 2003

1.	Smt Anju Bobby George	Athletics

DRONACHARYA AWARDS FOR 2003

1.	Shri Robert Bobby George	Athletics
2.	Shri Anoop Kumar	Boxing
3.	Shri Rajinder Singh	Hockey
4.	Shri Sukhchain Singh Cheema	Wrestling

ARJUNA AWARDS FOR 2003

1.	Km Soma Biswas	Athletics
2.	Smt Madhuri Saxena	Athletics
3.	Shri Pankaj Advani	Billiards and Snooker
4.	Km Mangte Chungneijang Marykom	Boxing
5.	Km Koneru Humpy	Chess
6.	Shri Harbhajan Singh	Cricket
7.	Km Mithali Raj	Cricket
8.	Capt Rajesh Pattu (SJRP)	Equestrian
9.	Shri Devesh Chauhan	Hockey
10.	Km. Suraj Lata Devi	Hockey

11.	Shri Akram Shah	Judo
12.	Shri Sanjeev Kumar	Kabaddi
13.	Major Rajyavardhan Singh Rathore	Shooting
14.	Shri Shokinder Tomar	Wrestling
15.	Shri Madasu Srinivas Rao	Badminton (Handicapped category)

DHYAN CHAND AWARDS FOR 2004

1.	Brig. (Retd.) Labh Singh	Athletics
2.	Shri Hardayal Singh	Hockey
3.	Shri Digambar P. Mehendale	Athletics (Handicapped Category)

MAULANA ABUL KALAM AZAD TROPHY 2002-2003

1. Guru Nanak Dev University, Amritsar

VIII. SELECTED INDIAN SPORTS PERSONALITIES

Sania Mirza (born November 15, 1986) is a professional female tennis player from India. She was born in Hyderabad, India.

Sania won the Wimbledon Championships Girls' Doubles title in 2003, teaming up with Alisa Kleybanova of Russia.

She got a wild card entry to the 2005 Australian Open and created history by becoming the first Indian woman to enter the third round of a Grand Slam tournament. She lost in the 3rd round to eventual champion Serena Williams. On February 12, 2005, she became the first Indian woman to win a WTA singles title defeating Alyona Bondarenko of Ukraine in the Hyderabad Open Finals.

- 2005 Dubai Tennis Championships: 2nd Round: Upset reigning US Open Champion Svetlana Kuznetsova 6-4, 6-2 to reach the quarter-finals.
- 2005 Hyderbad Open Singles: Won the tournament defeating Alyona Bodarenko of Ukraine 6-4, 5-7, 6-3 in the final and became the first Indian woman to capture a WTA singles title.
- 2005 Australian Open Singles: 3rd round: Became first Indian woman to reach the 3rd round of a Grand Slam tournament.
- 2004 Hyderabad Open Doubles: Won the tournament (partnering with Liezel Huber) to become the youngest Indian to win a WTA or ATP tour title and the first Indian woman to capture a WTA tour title.

2003 Junior Wimbledon Championships Doubles: Won the tournament (partnering with Alisa Kleybanova) to become the youngest Indian and the first Indian woman to win a junior Grand Slam title.

Rahul Dravid: the most steady batsman in the present Indian team was born in Indore on the 11th of January, 1973. He made his debut at Lord's in 1996 against England in the second Test and was unlucky not to score a century on debut. Before making his debut he was a well-known player in the local circuit having amassed tons of runs against all oppositions. Rahul Dravid has been one of the main pillars of the Indian batting with his blend of technical proficiency and stylish strokes. In a side packed with so many star batsmen, he has frequently played the sheet anchor role to perfection. The fact that most of his centuries have been scored outside India is a pointer to his unfaltering technique and temperament on all types of pitches. His style of batting was once regarded as too slow for the one day game, but through sheer practice; he has transformed himself into an integral part of the team in the shorter version of the game also. He was clearly the batsman of the 1999 World Cup with two hundreds and the highest aggregate. For sheer consistency, Dravid has few equals and has maintained a Test career average of over fifty. His temperament is exemplary and his concentration legendary. A batsman who revels in a crisis, Dravid, against New Zealand in January 1999, joined the ranks of Vijay Hazare and Sunil Gavaskar as one of only three Indians to have scored a century in each innings in a Test. He was chosen the Wisden Cricketer of the year for the year 2000.

Mahesh Bhupathi was born on the 6th of July 1974. He along with Leander Paes are responsible for bringing glory to the country umpteen number of times in world tennis. Mahesh was coached by his father right from his formative years. He became the first Indian to win a Grand Slam event when he won the mixed doubles crown in the French Open in 1998. Mahesh and Leander became the no. 1 pair in world tennis when they reached the finals of all the four Grand Slams in 1999, a record achievement wherein they won the French and Wimbledon Opens. But just when they started dominating the world tennis scene, they have decided to go their separate ways due to uncompromising differences and this is really a great blow to not only Indian tennis but the entire tennis world. The sooner they sort out the differences the better it will be for both of them and all their army of fans in the country for that they have got a lot more to give to Indian tennis. The best way would be to sit across the table and solve their problems without involving any third party as said by the Woodies, the great Australian pair who considered them to be their rightful heirs to dominate the world doubles scene like they did. Mahesh along with his father have now started a tennis village in Bangalore city to harness the tennis talent in the country. The tennis village has got world class facilities and tennis hopefuls of the country no longer have to look westwards to get coaching.

Vijay Amritraj (born December 14, 1953) is an Indian former tennis champion and actor. Amritraj and his brother, Anand Amritraj, were among the first Indians to play in an International tennis tournament. In 1976, the brothers were semi-finalists in the Wimbledon men's doubles. After retiring from the game in the 1980s, Vijay had a brief acting career, appearing with Roger Moore in the James Bond film, *Octopussy* and in *Star Trek IV: The Voyage Home*. He has since gone on to become a sports commentator, and has developed a successful multimedia business.

IX. OLYMPIC RINGS

The Olympic rings are the official symbol of the Olympic Games. There are five interlacing rings of colours—blue, yellow, black, green and red. The rings set upon a white background. The five rings represent the five continents.

X. PRESIDENTS OF INTERNATIONAL OLYMPIC COMMITTEE

Name	Country	Presidency
Demetrius Vikelas	Greece	1894-1896
Pierre de Coubertin	France	1896-1925
Henri de Baillet-Latour	Belgium	1925-1942
Sigfrid Edström	Sweden	1946-1952
Avery Brundage	United States	1952-1972
Lord Killanin	Ireland	1972-1980
Juan Antonio Samaranch	Spain	1980-2001
Jacques Rogge	Belgium	2001-

XI. LIST OF MEMBERS OF THE INTERNATIONAL OLYMPIC COMMITTEE

Member	Country	Since
Nawab Faisal Fahd Abdulaziz	Saudi Arabia	2002
Rubèn Acosta Hernández	Mexico	2000
Henry Adefope	Nigeria	1985
Tamás Aján	Hungary	2000
Prince Albert II	Monaco	1985
Shahid Ali	Pakistan	1996
Princess Anne	Great Britain	1988
Roland Baar	Germany	1999
Thomas Bach	Germany	1991
Sepp Blatter	Switzerland	1999
Valeri Borzov	Ukraine	1994
Fernando Bello	Portugal	1989
Els van Breda Vriesman	Netherlands	2001
Sergey Bubka	Ukraine	1999
Franco Carraro	Itlay	1982
Richard Carrión	Puerto Rico	1990
Manuela di Centa	Itlay	1999
Patrick Chamunda	Zambia	2002
Ottavio Cinquanta	Italy	1996
Chang Ung	North Korea	1996
John Coates	Australia	2001
Phil Coles	Australia	1982
Phil Craven	Great Britain	2003
Charmaine Crooks	Canada	1999
Bob Ctvrtlik	United States	1999
Anita DeFrantz	United States	1986
Lamine Diack	Senegal	1999
Alpha Ibrahim Diallo	Guinea	1994
Iván Dibos	Peru	1982
Guy Drut	France	1996
Jim Easton	United States	1994
Fransisco Elizalde	Philippines	1985
Manuel Estiarte	Spain	2000
René Fasel	Switzerland	1995
Nikos Filaretos	Greece	1981
Timothy Fok	Hong Kong	2001
Anton Geesink	Netherlands	1987
Alex Gilady	Israel	1994

Contd.

Contd.

Reynaldo González López	Cuba	1995
Richard Gosper	Australia	1977
Bruno Grandi	Itlay	2000
Tan Seri Hamzah bin	Malaysia	1978
Haji Abu Samah		
Bob Hasan	Indonesia	1994
Mostafa Hashemi Taba	Iran	2000
João Havelange	Brazil	1963
Issa Hayatou	Cameroon	2001
He Zhenliang	China	1981
Gerhard Heiberg	Norway	1994
Paul Henderson	Canada	2000
Grand Duke Henri	Luxembourg	1998
Patrick Hickey	Ireland	1995
Marc Hodler	Switzerland	1963
Kai Holm	Denmark	2002
Chiharu Igaya	Japan	1982
Nat Indrapana	Thailand	1990
Willi Kaltschmitt Luján	Guatemala	1988
Gian-Franco Kasper	Switzerland	2000
Kipchoge Keino	Kenya	2000
Toni Khoury	Lebanon	1995
Jean-Claude Killy	France	1995
Kim Un-Yong	South Korea	1986
Jari Kurri	Finland	2002
Mustapha Larfaoui	Algeria	1995
Lee Kun-Hee	South Korea	1996
Kikis Lazarides	Cyprus	2002
Gunilla Lindberg	Sweden	1996
Arne Ljungqvist	Sweden	1994
Julio César Maglione	Uruguay	1996
Shagdarjav Magvan	Mongolia	1977
Infanta Doña Pilar		
de Borbón	Spain	1996
Anani Matthia	Togo	1983
Fidel Mendoza Carrasquilla	Colombia	1988
Robin Mitchell	Fiji	1994
Samih Moudallal	Syria	1998
Nawal El Moutawakel	Morocco	1998
Roque Muñoz Peñá	Dominican Republic	1983
Mohamed Mzali	Tunisia	1965

Contd.

Contd.

François Narmon	Belgium	2002
Youssoupha Ndiaye	Senegal	2002
Ng Ser Miang	Singapore	1998
Lambris Nikolaou	Greece	1986
Princess Nora	Liechtenstein	1984
Carlos Nuzman	Brazil	2000
Francis Nyangweso	Uganda	1988
Shunichiro Okano	Japan	1990
Susie O'Neill	Australia	2000
Denis Oswald	Switzerland	1991
Lassana Palenfo	Côte d'Ivoire	2000
Park Yong Sung	South Korea	2002
Mario Pescante	Itlay	1994
Matthew Pinsent	Great Britain	2002
Aleksandr Popov	Russia	1999
Dick Pound	Canada	1978
Sam Ramswamy	South Africa	1995
Craig Reedie	Great Britain	1994
Antonio Rodriguez	Argentina	1990
Jacques Rogge	Belgium	1991
Ram Ruhee	Mauritius	1988
Ahmad Al-Sabah	Kuwait	1992
Mounir Sabet	Egypt	1998
Juan Antonio Samaranch Salisachs	Spain	2001
Melitón Sánchez Rivas	Panama	1998
Pá! Schmitt	Hungary	1983
Austin Sealy	Barbados	1994
Henri Sérandour	France	2000
Randhir Singh	India	2001
Ivan Slavkov	Bulgaria	1987
Vitali Smirnov	Russia	1971
Borislav Stankovic	Serbia and Montenegro	1988
Irena Szewinska	Poland	1998
Ådne Søndrål	Norway	2002
Peter Tallberg	Finland	1976
Shamil Tarpishchev	Russia	1994
Tamim bin Hamad Al-Thani	Qatar	2002
Walther Tröger	Germany	1989
Mario Vázquez Raña	Mexico	1991
Olegario Vázquez Raña	Mexico	1995

Contd.

Contd.

Hein Verbruggen	Netherlands	1996
Antun Vrdoljak	Croatia	1995
Leo Wallner	Austria	1998
Pernilla Wiberg	Sweden	2002
Prince Willem-Alexander	Netherlands	1998
Tay Wilson	New Zealand	1988
Wu Ching-Kuo	Chinese Taipei	1988
Yu Zaiqing	China	2000

XII. VENUE OF WINTER OLYMPIC GAMES

Years	Venue	Country
1924	Chamonix	France
1928	St. Mortiz	Switzerland
1932	Lake Placid New York	U.S.A.
1936	Garmisch Partenkirchen	Germany
1948	St. Mortiz	Switzerland
1952	Oslo	Norway
1956	Cortina D' Ampezzo	Italy
1960	Squaw Valley California	U.S.A.
1964	Innsbruck	Austria
1968	Grenoble	France
1972	Sapporo	Japan
1976	Innsbruck	Austria
1984	Lake Placid New York	U.S.A.
1988	Calgary	Canada
1992	Albertville	France
1994	Lillehammer	Norway
1998	Nagono	Japan
2002	Salt Lake City	U.S.A.
2006	Turin	Italy (Scheduled)

XIII. OLYMPICS AT GLANCE

Olympic Games	Year	Host City	Nation with Max. Medals
The First Olympic Games	1896	Athens	47 Greece
The Second Olympic Games	1900	Paris	102 France

Contd.

Contd.

The Third Olympic Games	1904	St. Louis	238 USA
The Fourth Olympic Games	1908	London	145 Britain
The Fifth Olympic Games	1912	Stockholm	65 Sweden
The Sixth Olympic Games	1916	*Cancelled due to World War-I*	
The Seventh Olympic Games	1920	Antwerp	96 USA
The Eighth Olympic Games	1924	Paris	99 USA
The Ninth Olympic Games	1928	Amsterdam	56 USA
The Tenth Olympic Games	1932	Los Angeles	104 USA
The Eleventh Olympic Games	1936	Berlin	89 E. Germany
The Twelfth Olympic Games	1940	*Cancelled due to World War-II*	
The Thirteenth Olympic Games	1944	*Cancelled due to World War-II*	
The Fourteenth Olympic Games	1948	London	84 USA
The Fifteenth Olympic Games	1952	Helsinki	76 USA
The Sixteenth Olympic Games	1956	Melbourne	98 USSR
The Seventeenth Olympic Games	1960	Rome	103 USSR
The Eighteenth Olympic Games	1964	Tokyo	90 USA
The Nineteenth Olympic Games	1968	Mexico City	107 USA
The Twentieth Olympic Games	1972	Munich	99 USSR
The Twenty-First Olympic Games	1976	Montreal	125 USSR
The Twenty-Second Olympic Games	1980	Moscow	195 USSR
The Twenty-Third Olympic Games	1984	Los angeles	174 USA
The Twenty-Fourth Olympic Games	1988	Seoul	132 USSR
The Twenty-Fifth Olympic Games	1992	Barcelona	112 United Team
The Twenty-Sixth Olympic Games	1996	Atlanta	101 USA
The Twenty-Seventh Olympic Games	2000	Sydney	97 USA
The Twenty-Eighth Olympic Games	2004	Athens	88 USA
The Twenty-Ninth Olympic Games	2008	Beijing (China)	Scheduled

XIV. VENUE OF COMMONWEALTH GAMES

Years	Venue	Country
1930	Hamilton	Canada
1934	London	U.K.
1938	Sydney	Australia
1950	Auckland	New Zealand
1954	Vancouver	Canada
1958	Cardiff	U.K.
1962	Perth	Australia
1966	Jamaica	West Indies
1970	Edinburgh	U.K.
1974	Christchurch	New Zealand

Contd.

Contd.

1978	Edmoton	Canada
1982	Brisbane	Australia
1986	Edinburgh	U.K.
1990	Auckland	New Zealand
1994	Victoria	Canada
1998	Kuala Lumpur	Malaysia
2002	Manchester	U.K.
2006	Melbourne	Australia (Scheduled)
2010	Delhi	India (Scheduled)

XV. ASIAN GAMES

The **Asian Games**, also called the **Asiad**, is a multi-sport event held every four years among athletes from all over Asia.

1. 1951 Asian Games, New Delhi, India
2. 1954 Asian Games, Manila, Philippines
3. 1958 Asian Games, Tokyo, Japan
4. 1962 Asian Games, Jakarta, Indonesia
5. 1966 Asian Games, Bangkok, Thailand
6. 1970 Asian Games, Bangkok, Thailand
7. 1974 Asian Games, Tehran, Iran
8. 1978 Asian Games, Bangkok, Thailand
9. 1982 Asian Games, New Delhi, India
10. 1986 Asian Games, Seoul, South Korea
11. 1990 Asian Games, Beijing, People's Republic of China
12. 1994 Asian Games, Hiroshima, Japan
13. 1998 Asian Games, Bangkok, Thailand
14. 2002 Asian Games, Busan, South Korea
15. 2006 Asian Games, Doha, Qatar December 1-15 (Scheduled)
16. 2010 Asian Games, Guangzhou, People's Republic of China (Scheduled).

XVI. WINTER ASIAN GAMES

1. 1986 Winter Asian Games, Sapporo, Japan
2. 1990 Winter Asian Games, Sapporo, Japan
3. 1996 Winter Asian Games, Harbin, People's Republic of China
4. 1999 Winter Asian Games, Kangwon, South Korea

5. 2003 Winter Asian Games, Aomori, Japan
6. 2007 Winter Asian Games, Changchun, People's Republic of China (Scheduled)
7. 2011 Winter Asian Games, Beirut, Lebanon (Scheduled).

XVII. WORLD CUP CRICKET

Years	Venue	Winner	Runner-ups
1975	U.K.	West Indies	Australia
1979	U.K.	West Indies	England
1983	U.K.	India	West Indies
1987	India and Pakistan	Australia	England
1991-92	Australia	Pakistan	England
1996	India, Pakistan and Sri Lanka	Srilanka	Australia
1999	England	Australia	Pakistan
2003	S. Africa	Australia	India
2007	West Indies (Scheduled)		

XVIII. WORLD CUP HOCKEY

Years	Winner	Runner-up
1971	Pakistan	Spain
1973	Holland	India
1975	India	Pakistan
1978	Pakistan	Holland
1982	Pakistan	West Germany
1986	Australia	England
1990	Holland	Pakistan
1994	Pakistan	Australia
1998	Holland	Spain
2002	Germany	Australia
2006		

XIX. WORLD CUP FOOTBALL

Years	Venue	Winner	Runner-ups
1930	Uruguay	Uruguay	Argentina
1934	Italy	Italy	Czechoslovakia
1938	France	Italy	Hungary
1942*	–	–	–

Contd.

Contd.

1946*	–	–	–
1950	Brazil	Uruguay	Brazil
1954	Switzerland	West Germany	Hungary
1958	Sweden	Brazil	Sweden
1962	Chile	Brazil	Czechoslovakia
1966	England	England	West Germany
1970	Mexico	Brazil	Italy
1974	West Germany	West Germany	Netherlands
1978	Argentina	Argentina	Netherlands
1982	Spain	Italy	West Germany
1986	Mexico	Argentina	West Germany
1990	Italy	West Germany	Argentina
1994	U.S.A.	Brazil	Italy
1998	France	France	Brazil
2002	Japan and S. Korea	Brazil	Germany
2006	Germany (Scheduled)		

* Not played

XX. CAREERS RELATED TO SPORT AND FITNESS

Source: Sport Administration Manual 1999, IOC, Switzerland

Sports Science and Medicine

- Centre Director
- Sports Chiropractor
- Athletic Therapist
- Massage Therapist
- Orthopedic Surgeon
- Pediatric Orthopedic Surgeon
- Sports Medicine Specialist
- General Practitioner (Community Sports Medicine)
- Sports Medicine (Epidemiology/Scientist)
- Nutritionist
- Orthotist
- Physiologist
- Biomechanics Specialist
- Biochemist

- Physiotherapist
- Growth and Development Specialist
- Sports Psychologist
- Laboratory Assistant
- Kinesiologist/Physical Educator (Fitness/Lifestyle)
- Kinesiologist/Physical Educator (Exercise/Stress Testing)
- Personal Trainer/Fitness Instructor
- Nurse
- Computer Programmer/System Analyst
- Record Technician
- Receptionist

Sports and Fitness

- High Performance
  - National Team Director
  - Coach
  - Assistant Coach
  - Trainer/Athletic Therapist
  - High Performance Program Director
  - Technical Director
  - Administrative Assistant
- Recreation, Fitness and Lifestyle
  - Fitness Centre Director
  - Owner, Private Club
  - Aerobics/Fitness Instructor
  - Personal Trainer
  - Diet and Nutrition Counsellor
  - Recreation Administration
  - Manager/Director of Facilities Operations
  - Pro Shop Manager/Director
- Manager Director of Customer and Corporate Relations
- Merchandising Director
- Program Director
  - Outdoor Program Director
  - Manager of Racquet Courts
  - Manager, Fitness and Lifestyle Centre
  - Programmer/Analyst

- Budget Officer
- Marketing Coordinator

Sport Administration (national to club level)
- Executive Director
- Program Director
- Marketing Director
- Communications Director
- Membership Director
- Sport Consultant
- Museum Administrator

Professional Sports

- President and CEO
- Executive Vice President
- Vice President, Finance and Administration
- Vice President, Marketing and Broadcasting
- General Manager
- Director of Operations
- Scout
- Head Coach
- Assistant Coach
- Professional Athlete
- Team Trainer
- Equipment Manager
- Director, Public Relations
- Manager, Marketing and Special Events
- Director, Sales and Licensing
- Director, Advertising and Publishing
- Office Manager
- Director of Ticket Operations/Ticket Manager
- Manager, Corporate Resources
- Controller
- League Operations
- President, Players Association
- League Commissioner
- Referee/Umpire
- Game Officials
- Promotions and Advertising Manager/Director

Sports Marketing and Event Management

- Sport Marketing
- Player Agent
- Player Marketing Representative
- Endorsements Agent
- Director of Public Relations
- Players Union Negotiator
- Lawyer
- Fund Raising, Public Solicitation
- Licensing/Sponsorship Consultant
- Television Consultant, Sports
- Sports Personality
- Event management (e.g., hosting an Olympic Games)
- President and CEO
- Vice President, Games
- Vice President, Finance and Controls
- Manager/Director, Sports
- Schedule and Planning Director
- Event Organiser
  - Venue Design and Construction Director
  - Village Design and Services Director
  - Security Director
  - Logistics Director
  - Medical Services Director
  - Manager/Director, Games Services
  - Ceremonies Director
  - Image Director
  - Publications Director
  - Promotions Director
  - Manager/Director, Olympic Broadcast Organization (Host Broadcasting)
  - Manager/Director, Support Services
  - Human Resources Director
  - Volunteer Programs Director
  - Community Affairs Director

The Business of Sports

- Sports Travel/Tours Coordinator
- Owner/Manager, Sport, Bar
- Programmer (Computer/Electronic Games)

Sports Media

- Journalist
- Reporter (television, radio, print)
- Photographer
- Camera Operator
- Video Editor
- Control Room Operators
- Producer
- Director
- Play-by-Play Announcer
- Colour Commentator
- Content providers for sports-oriented websites
- See also Host Broadcasting in Event Management

Sporting Goods

- Engineering Manager
- Director of Research and Development
- Product Designer
- Director of Marketing
- Regional Sales Representative
- Account Executive
- Commercial Equipment Representative
- Store Manager

University and College Athletics

- Athletic Director
- Budget Officer
- Sports and Information Director
- Marketing and Promotions Officer
- Sponsorship Manager
- Coaches

- Trainer/Athletic Therapist
- Strength/Conditioning Coach
- Travel Coordinator
- Campus Recreation (link to Fitness and Lifestyle)
- Physical Education (possible areas)
- Outdoor Recreation
- Business and Sport
- Dance Education
- Teacher Training
- Teacher (various disciplines).